Focus on Grammar

An **INTRODUCTORY** Course for Reference and Practice

Samuela Eckstut

Longman

FOCUS ON GRAMMAR WORKBOOK: AN INTRODUCTORY COURSE FOR REFERENCE AND PRACTICE

Pearson Education, 10 Bank Street, White Plains, NY 10606

Senior Acquisitions Editor: Laura LeDrean
Development Director: Penny Laporte
Director of design and production: Rhea Banker
Development editors: Stacey Hunter, Karen Davy
Production manager: Liza Pleva
Managing editor: Linda Moser
Production editor: Marc Oliver
Director of manufacturing: Patrice Fraccio
Senior manufacturing buyer: David Dickey
Photo research: Dana Klinek
Cover design: Rhea Banker
Text design adaptation: Rainbow Graphics
Project management and text composition: Proof Positive/Farrowlyne Associates, Inc.
Illustrators: Paul McCusker: pp. 7, 67, 81, 125, 180; Andy Myer: pp. 1–2, 4–6, 12–17, 19–20, 24, 34–37, 42, 44, 46–47, 49, 51–53, 55–56, 60–61, 69, 74, 79, 83, 88–89, 94, 104, 112–114, 123, 128, 130, 132–133, 141, 146, 150, 155–156, 160, 165–166, 170, 174–175, 183; Dusan Petricic: pp. 2, 71, 80, 101–102, 129, 152, 163; Tom Sperling: p. 58.

Photo credits: **p. 7** *(left)* © Corbis/Mitchell Gerber, *(center)* Everett Collection, *(right)* Associated Press AP; **p. 8** *(top left)* Reuters/Yves Herman/Hulton/Archive, *(top center)* Associated Press AP, *(top right)* IHA/AP/Wide World Photos, *(bottom left)* © Corbis/Mitchell Gerber, *(bottom center)* Corbis, *(bottom right)* © Corbis/Bettmann; **p. 25** *(a.)* © Corbis/Chuck Savage, *(b.)* © Spencer Grant/PhotoEdit, *(c.)* © Michael Newman/PhotoEdit, *(d.)* © Corbis/Tom & Dee Ann McCarthy; **p. 26** *(e.)* © Corbis/Richard Cummins, *(f.)* © Tony Freeman/PhotoEdit, *(g.)* Tom Carter/PhotoEdit, *(h.)* © Corbis/Peter Turnley, *(i.)* © Corbis/Royalty-Free, *(j.)* © Michael Newman/PhotoEdit, *(k.)* © Corbis/Jose Luis Pelaez, Inc., *(l.)* © Tony Freeman/PhotoEdit; **p. 72** *(left)* AP/Wide World Photos, *(right)* AP/Wide World Photos; **p. 90** *(top left)* © Corbis/Robert Landau, *(bottom left)* © David Young-Wolff/PhotoEdit, *(top right)* Photo of Spencer shoes courtesy of Allen-Edmonds Shoe Corporation, *(bottom right)* RoadRunnerSports.com; **p. 91** *(bottom left)* © Michael Newman/PhotoEdit, *(top left)* AP/Wide World Photos, *(top right)* © www.shadesoffun.com, *(bottom right)* © Corbis/Royalty-Free; **p. 143** *(top left)* © Courtesy of Mercedes-Benz USA, LLC, *(top center)* Photo courtesy of Frank Zimmerman, *(top right)* © Michael Newman/PhotoEdit, *(middle left)* © Corbis/Tibor Bognar, *(middle center)* © Corbis/Royalty-Free, *(middle right)* © Corbis/Bill Ross, *(bottom left)* © Corbis/Paul A. Souders, *(bottom center)* © Corbis/Charles O'Rear, *(bottom right)* © Corbis/Carl & Ann Purcell; **p. 144** *(left)* Bernard Gotfryd/Hulton/Archive, *(center)* Associated Press AP, *(right)* © Corbis/Bettmann; **p. 178** *(top left)* © Corbis/Richard Cummins, *(top right)* © Corbis/Peter Turnley, *(bottom left)* © Corbis/Tom & Dee Ann McCarthy, *(bottom right)* © Corbis/Patrik Giardino.

ISBN: 0–13–111781–5

1 2 3 4 5 6 7 8 9 10—BAH—08 07 06 05 04 03

CONTENTS

ABOUT THE AUTHOR

Samuela Eckstut has taught ESL and EFL for twenty-five years, in the United States, Greece, Italy, and England. Currently she is teaching at Boston University, Center for English Language and Orientation Programs (CELOP). She has authored or co-authored numerous texts for the teaching of English, notably *What's in a Word? Reading and Vocabulary Building*; *In the Real World*; *First Impressions*; *Beneath the Surface*; *Widely Read*; *Finishing Touches*; and *Strategic Reading*.

IMPERATIVES

 AFFIRMATIVE AND NEGATIVE IMPERATIVES

Look at the pictures. What are the people saying? Circle the correct answers.

1. a. Move.
   b. Don't move.

2. a. Sit down.
   b. Don't sit down.

3. a. Close your books.
   b. Don't close your books.

4. a. Be nervous.
   b. Don't be nervous.

5. a. Be good.
   b. Don't be good.

6. a. Open your eyes.
   b. Don't open your eyes.

2 INSTRUCTIONS

Write instructions. Use the words in the box.

Answer	Ask	Close	Listen to	Look at	Open	Read

1. _____Read_____ the book.

_____Open_____

_____

_____

2. _____ the CD.

_____

3. _____ the board.

_____

4. _____ the teacher.

_____

_____

_____

5. _____ the group.

_____

_____

6. _____ the window.

❸ NUMBERS (1–10)

Complete the sentences. Write the numbers.

$$\begin{array}{r} 1 \\ +1 \\ \hline 2 \end{array} \qquad \begin{array}{r} 5 \\ +3 \\ \hline 8 \end{array}$$

1. One and one is ____two____.

2. _____ and three is eight.

3. Three and _____ is ten.

4. Nine and one is _____.

5. Two and six is _____.

6. Three and _____ is six.

7. _____ and five is six.

8. Seven and two is _____.

9. _____ and three is nine.

10. Three and _____ is seven.

❹ EDITING

Correct the conversations. There is one mistake in each conversation.

1. **A:** Sorry.

   B: ~~That~~ That's okay.

2. **A:** Hi. I Maria Sanchez.

   B: Nice to meet you.

3. **A:** How you are?

   B: Not so good.

4. **A:** Can I sit here?

   B: Sure. Sit please down.

5 CONVERSATION COMPLETION

Complete the conversation. Use the words in the box. (Don't look at pages 4–5 in your Student Book.)

Bye	how	Listen	Nice	tape
Don't	I'm	nervous	~~Please~~	teacher

STEVE: Can I sit here?

JUDY: Sure. ___Please___ sit down.
1.

STEVE: Hi, I'm Steve Beck.

JUDY: _____ to meet you. _____
2.   3.
Judy Johnson.

STEVE: Oops! Sorry.

JUDY: That's okay. Nervous?

STEVE: I guess so. It's my first day here. I'm a new

_____.
4.

JUDY: Oh. Don't be _____ . . .
5.

JUDY: Here. _____ to this.
6.

STEVE: What is it?

JUDY: A _____.
7.

STEVE: Uh . . . No thanks.

JUDY: Try it. It's short. It's fun. [*Joking*] And it's free.

STEVE: Well, okay.

JUDY: Well, _____ are you now?
8.

STEVE: Good.

JUDY: _____ worry. Repeat ten times, "I'm a
9.

good teacher." And have a good class.

STEVE: Okay, Judy. Thanks. _____.
10.

2 THIS IS / THESE ARE; SUBJECT PRONOUNS

1 WORDS

Look at the picture of Marsha's family. Match the letter with the correct description. The first one is done for you.

_c_ **1.** Hi, I'm Marsha. This is me.

____ **2.** This is my husband, Sam.

____ **3.** These are my parents.

____ **4.** This is my brother.

____ **5.** This is my son.

____ **6.** This is my daughter.

____ **7.** These are my sisters.

____ **8.** These are my children.

2 VOCABULARY

Complete the crossword puzzle.

ACROSS

2.

7.

8.

9.

10.

11.

12.

13.

DOWN

1.

3.

4.

5.

6. 

9. (pens image)

❸ SUBJECT PRONOUNS

Complete the sentences with **I**, **you**, **he**, **she**, **it**, **we**, *or* **they**.

Marie-Claire is my friend. _____*She*_____ is from Quebec. Quebec is a city in Canada.
1.

_____ is a nice city. Marie-Claire says, "_____ love Quebec.
2. 3.

_____ is my home." _____ lives in Quebec with her husband, Eric.
4. 5.

_____ is from New York. _____ are teachers. The school is near their
6. 7.

home. _____ is a big school. Eric says, "_____ are new teachers. Our
8. 9.

students are new too. _____ are very nice."
10.

❹ THIS IS / THESE ARE

Look at the pictures and the names in the box. Write sentences. Use **this is** *or* **these are**.

Louis Armstrong	Céline Dion	Emperor Akihito and Empress Michiko
Jackie Chan	Albert Einstein	Prince William and Prince Harry
Cameron Diaz	~~Salma Hayek~~	Venus and Serena Williams

1.

2.

3.

1. This is Salma Hayek.

2. _____

3. _____

(continued on next page)

4.

_____

_____

5.

_____

_____

6.

_____

_____

7.

_____

_____

8.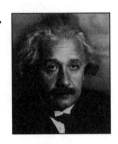

_____

_____

9.

_____

_____

⑤ THIS IS / THESE ARE

Put the words in the correct order. Write sentences.

1. book / this / your / is / ?   Is this your book?_____

2. book / this / your / is / .   _____

3. your / is / ticket / this / ?   _____

4. keys / are/ these / your / .   _____

5. my / is / house / this / .   _____

6. is / apartment / your / this / ?   _____

7. your / these / friends / are / ?   _____

8. these / seats / your / are / .   _____

6 THIS IS / THESE ARE

Complete the sentences. Circle the correct answers and write them on the lines.

1. These are my ____parents____.

   a. parent   **(b.)** parents

2. This is my _____.

   a. brother   **b.** brothers

3. These are my _____.

   a. sister   **b.** sisters

4. These are my _____.

   a. friend   **b.** friends

5. This is my _____.

   a. partner   **b.** partners

6. This is my _____.

   a. class   **b.** classes

7 EDITING

Correct the conversations. There is one mistake in each conversation.

1. **A:** Is ~~these~~ this your ticket?

   B: Yes, it is.

2. **A:** These are your keys?

   B: Yes. Thank you.

3. **A:** This is my car.

   B: She is big.

4. **A:** This are my books.

   B: Oh. Sorry.

5. **A:** These are my pet.

   B: They're nice.

6. **A:** Is this your sister?

   B: Yes, her name is Mary. He is a teacher.

UNIT

3

THE PRESENT OF *BE*: STATEMENTS

1 AFFIRMATIVE AND NEGATIVE STATEMENTS WITH *BE*

Read the class list. Put a check (**) next to the statements that are true.

CLASS LIST			
Abdullah al-Karim	Egypt	Gabriella Ravela	Italy
Huang-Ping Cho	Taiwan	José Rodriguez	Mexico
Deng-Tsao Hu	Taiwan	Fatima Sanaifi	Egypt
Ana Leite	Brazil	Guadalupe Sanchez	Mexico
Peter Lundgren	the United States	Antonio Villanueva	Peru
Susan O'Neill	Australia	Yoshi Yamomoto	Japan

_____ 1. I'm Yoshi Yamomoto. I'm from the United States.

_____ 2. This is Peter Lundgren. He isn't from Australia.

_____ 3. I'm Antonio Villanueva. I'm not from Peru.

_____ 4. These are Guadalupe Sanchez and José Rodriguez. They're from Mexico.

_____ 5. I'm Deng-Tsao Hu and this is Huang-Ping Cho. We're not from Japan.

_____ 6. This is Susan O'Neill. She's from the United States.

_____ 7. This is Gabriella Ravela. She isn't from Italy.

_____ 8. This is Ana Leite. She's not from Mexico.

_____ 9. These are Abdullah al-Karim and Fatima Sanaifi. They aren't from Egypt.

2 AFFIRMATIVE AND NEGATIVE STATEMENTS WITH *BE*

Complete the sentences. Use **is** *or* **isn't**.

1. New York ____isn't____ the capital of the United States.

2. Brasília ____is____ the capital of Brazil.

3. Sydney _____ the capital of Australia.

4. Quebec _____ the capital of Canada.

5. Cairo _____ the capital of Egypt.

6. Rome _____ the capital of Italy.

7. Canberra _____ the capital of Austria.

8. Tokyo _____ the capital of Japan.

3 AFFIRMATIVE STATEMENTS WITH *BE*

Complete the letter. Use **am**, **is**, *or* **are**.

January 21

Dear Mom and Dad,

    Karen and I ____are____ *in Sydney. It* _____ *warm here. It*
          1.   2.
_____ *32°C today. Sydney* _____ *a wonderful city. The Opera*
   3.   4.
House _____ *beautiful, and the people* _____ *friendly.*
       5.   6.
    We _____ *at the Canberra Hotel. The rooms* _____ *big but a*
       7.   8.
little expensive. Karen _____ *in the hotel room now. I* _____ *at*
                9.   10.
a very nice restaurant. The food _____ *delicious.*
                11.

                        Love,

                        Paul

4 **CONTRACTIONS OF AFFIRMATIVE AND NEGATIVE STATEMENTS WITH *BE***

Write the sentences in full form.

1. I'm happy here. __I am happy here.__

2. It's beautiful. _____

3. She isn't cold. _____

4. We're not on vacation. _____

5. They're nice. _____

6. You aren't from here. _____

5 **CONTRACTIONS OF AFFIRMATIVE AND NEGATIVE STATEMENTS WITH *BE***

Write the sentences with contractions.

1. It is not hot. __It's not hot. (OR: It isn't hot.)__

2. We are from Tokyo. _____

3. They are not here. _____

4. I am not the teacher. _____

5. He is my cousin. _____

6. You are not noisy. _____

6 **AFFIRMATIVE AND NEGATIVE STATEMENTS WITH *BE***

Complete the sentences. Use **'m**, **'m not**, **'s**, **isn't** *(or* **'s not***),* **'re**, **aren't** *(or* **'re not***).*

1. We __aren't__ hot.

We __'re__ cold.

2. They _____ happy.

They _____ sad.

3. The room _____ clean.

It _____ dirty.

4. The car _____ big.

It _____ small.

5. The food _____ delicious.

It _____ awful.

6. I _____ in Room 202.

I _____ in Room 101.

 **EDITING**

Correct the conversations. There are two mistakes in each conversation.

1. A: ~~Are~~ Is Mark from around here?

  B: Yes, ~~they~~ he is.

2. A: The food good?

  B: Is delicious.

3. A: This my cousin.

  B: Are she a student?

4. A: Be you from Mexico?

  B: No, we're are from Peru.

5. A: Your cousins Amy and Mary are here on vacation?

  B: No, they here on business.

8 CONVERSATION COMPLETION

Complete the conversation. Use the words in the box. (Don't look at pages 18–19 in your Student Book.)

am	capital	opera	too
are	is	They're	We're
Australia	not	~~this~~	you

MARK: Hi, Steve.

STEVE: Hi, Mark. Mark, _____this_____ is my cousin Amy, and this _____ her
        _{1.}   _{2.}
        friend Jenny. _____ here on vacation.
                      _{3.}

MARK: Hi. Nice to meet you.

AMY: Nice to meet you _____.
                          _{4.}

MARK: So you're _____ from around here?
                    _{5.}

AMY: No. We're from _____.
                        _{6.}

MARK: Australia? Ah—the land of kangaroos and koalas.

AMY: And big business, and _____, and . . .
                              _{7.}

MARK: Right. Are you from the _____?
                                 _{8.}

AMY: No. _____ from Sydney. And our kangaroos and koalas _____
            _{9.}   _{10.}
        all . . .

MARK: In the zoo?

AMY: That's right. Are _____ from Seattle?
                          _{11.}

MARK: Yes, I _____.
                 _{12.}

THAT IS / THOSE ARE; POSSESSIVE ADJECTIVES; PLURAL NOUNS

1 WORDS AND EXPRESSIONS

Look at the pictures. Read Annie's sentences about her family. Circle the correct answers.

1. **a.** That's me and my brother. His name's Jeremy.

   (b.) That's me and my brothers. Their names are Jeremy and Ben.

2. **a.** That's our house.

   b. That's their house.

3. **a.** That's my grandfather. His name's Bill.

   b. Those are my grandparents. Her name's Mary and his name's Bill.

4. **a.** That's our house.

   b. That's their house.

② POSSESSIVE ADJECTIVES

Look at the pictures. Write Annie's sentences about her family.

1. _That's my mother._

2. _____ Jessica.

3. _____

4. _____ Tim.

③ SINGULAR AND PLURAL NOUNS

Write the sentences in the singular.

1. Those women are from Brazil. _That woman is from Brazil._

2. Those cars are from Italy. _____

3. Those children are from Canada. _____

4. Those boys are from Egypt. _____

5. Those dishes are from Austria. _____

④ SINGULAR AND PLURAL NOUNS

Write the sentences in the plural.

1. That woman is from Brazil. _Those women are from Brazil._

2. That person is from Mexico. _____

3. That girl is from Japan. _____

4. That glass is from Australia. _____

5. That computer is from the United States. _____

5 POSSESSIVE ADJECTIVES

Complete the story. Use **my**, **his**, **her**, **our**, *or* **their**.

That's me and _____my_____ family.
 1.

Those are _____ sisters.
 2.

_____ names are Kate, Ann, and
 3.

Ruth. And that's _____ little
 4.

brother. _____ name is Sam.
 5.

_____ parents aren't in the
 6.

picture. Kate and _____ husband
 7.

have one daughter. _____ name
 8.

is Amy.

6 SUBJECT PRONOUNS AND POSSESSIVE ADJECTIVES

Complete the conversations. Circle the correct answers and write them on the lines.

1. A: My name's Serena.

   B: _____ a beautiful name.

   a. Its   **(b.)** It's

2. A: _____ wrong.

   a. Your   **b.** You're

   B: No, I'm not.

3. A: Tim and Jessica aren't here.

   B: But _____ car is here.

   a. their   **b.** they're

(continued on next page)

4. A: _____ car's nice.

   a. Your   **b.** You're

B: Thanks.

5. A: Are those your CDs?

   B: No, _____ my brother's CDs.

   a. their   **b.** they're

6. A: Is that your cat?

   B: Yes, _____ name is Ernie.

   a. its   **b.** it's

7 EDITING

Correct the conversations. There are two mistakes in each conversation.

1. A: Is that your ~~books~~?   *book*

   B: Yes, ~~its~~ is.   *it*

2. A: Are those you're children?

   B: No, they're our grandchild.

3. A: Are that your glasses?

   B: No, they're my sunglass.

4. A: Those person are teachers.

   B: His names are Steve Beck and Annie Macintosh.

5. A: That is your granddaughter?

   B: Yes, she name's Jessica.

8 CONVERSATION COMPLETION

Complete the conversation. Use the words in the box. (Don't look at pages 24–25 in your Student Book.)

grandchildren	her	Its	that
granddaughter	He's	It's	their
grandson	His	My	~~those~~

ROSE: Okay. So who are ___those___ people?
1.

MARY: _____ daughter, Jessica, and
2.

_____ husband, Tim. That's their
3.

house. Okay . . . Now here's the next slide.

ROSE: Is that _____ car? Look!
4.

_____ tires are flat.
5.

MARY: Well, it's Tim's car. _____ his "baby."
6.

He's fixing it. That's Tim under the car.

ROSE: And who are the kids?

MARY: They're my _____.
7.

ROSE: What? You're a grandparent?

MARY: I sure am. That's Annie, my _____.
8

And that's Ben, my younger grandson.

ROSE: And who's _____ guy?
9.

MARY: That's Jeremy, my older _____.
10.

_____ favorite things are computers
11.

and CDs. _____ a great kid!
12.

5 THE PRESENT OF *BE*: YES / NO QUESTIONS; QUESTIONS WITH *WHO* AND *WHAT*

1 **YES / NO QUESTIONS WITH *BE*;**
QUESTIONS WITH *WHO* AND *WHAT*

Write two conversations. Use the sentences in the box.

> Diaz.
> No, she isn't.
> She's a writer.
> No, that's my sister Kathy.
> Yes, she is. She's very nice.
> Oh. She's my teacher. Her name's Amy.
> Is she friendly?
> Is she famous?
> Is ~~that your~~ wife?
> What does she do?
> Wh~~o's that wo~~man?
> What's her last name?

Conversation 1

A: Who's that woman?

B: _____

A: _____

B: _____

A: _____

B: _____

Conversation 2

A: Is that your wife?

B: _____

A: _____

B: _____

A: _____

B: _____

2 WORDS AND EXPRESSIONS

Complete the sentences. Use the names of famous people.

1. _____Antonio Banderas_____ is an actor.

2. _____ is an actress.

3. _____ is an athlete.

4. _____ is a scientist.

5. _____ is an athlete.

6. _____ is an actor from my country.

3 YES / NO QUESTIONS WITH BE

Complete the conversations with questions. Use the words in parentheses.

1. **A:** I'm not a teacher.

   B: Oh. __Are you a student?_____
                     (you / a student)

2. **A:** She's not my cousin.

   B: Oh. _____
                     (she / your sister)

3. **A:** They're not from Mexico.

   B: Oh. _____
                     (they / from Peru)

4. **A:** He isn't a singer.

   B: Oh. _____
                     (he / an actor)

5. **A:** Their last name isn't Wilson.

   B: Oh. _____
                     (it / Woolson)

6. **A:** I'm not Josh.

   B: Oh. _____
                     (you / Joe)

7. **A:** Jessica and Ken aren't here on vacation.

   B: Oh. _____
                     (they / here on business)

4 SHORT ANSWERS WITH THE PRESENT OF *BE*

Answer the questions. Write true short answers.

1. Are you a student?

Yes, I am.

2. Are you single?

_____

3. Are you nervous?

_____

4. Is your teacher married?

_____

5. Is your teacher from Canada?

_____

6. Is it hot now?

_____

7. Are your classmates famous?

_____

8. Are you and your classmates from Brazil?

_____

5 QUESTIONS WITH *WHO* AND *WHAT*

Complete the chart. Write short answers.

	QUESTIONS	LONG ANSWERS	SHORT ANSWERS
1.	What's your name?	It's Mary.	Mary.
2.	Who's that student?	That's Ben.	
3.	Who are they?	They're my grandchildren.	
4.	What's that?	It's a key.	

6 QUESTIONS WITH *WHO* AND *WHAT*

Complete the chart. Write long answers.

	QUESTIONS	SHORT ANSWERS	LONG ANSWERS
1.	What's your name?	Mary.	It's Mary.
2.	Who's that man?	My brother.	
3.	What's the capital of Australia?	Canberra.	
4.	Who's the teacher of this class?	Lynn Martin.	

7 EDITING

Correct the conversations. There are nine mistakes. The first one is corrected for you.

1. **A:** ~~Who's~~ What's her last name?

   B: Martinez.

2. **A:** You and Joe married?

   B: No, we're not.

3. **A:** Who be that boy?

   B: That my son.

4. **A:** Who is the capital of the United States?

   B: Is Washington, D.C.

5. **A:** That woman your mother?

   B: Yes, she's.

6. **A:** Bob a travel agent is?

   B: No, he isn't.

⑧ CONVERSATION COMPLETION

Complete the conversations. Use the words in the box. (Don't look at page 30 in your Student Book.)

~~Are~~	He's	she	Who's
does	Is	she's	Yes
Her	it	What	you

STEVE: Mark?

MARK: Steve! _____Are_____ you here for the
1.
wedding?

STEVE: Yes, I am. Amanda is my cousin. What

about _____?
2.

MARK: Josh and I are good friends from school.
It's a great wedding, isn't it?

STEVE: Yes, _____ is.
3.

★

KATHY: _____ that man with Steve?
4.

AMANDA: His name is Mark. He and Josh are friends.

KATHY: Hmm. _____ he single?
5.

AMANDA: _____, he is.
6.

KATHY: What _____ he do?
7.

AMANDA: _____ a writer. He writes travel
8.
books.

KATHY: Oh.

★

MARK: Who's that woman with Amanda?

STEVE: _____ name is Kathy.
9.

MARK: Is _____ married?
10.

STEVE: No, _____ not.
11.

MARK: _____ does she do?
12.

STEVE: She's a travel agent.

MARK: Oh.

THE PRESENT OF *BE*: QUESTIONS WITH *WHERE*; PREPOSITIONS OF PLACE

1 WORDS AND EXPRESSIONS

Unscramble the words. Then match the words with the pictures.

___c___ **1.** tapnarmet libgundi   _____apartment building_____

_____ **2.** restkemruap   _____

_____ **3.** eviom ratheet   _____

_____ **4.** birlyar   _____

_____ **5.** sutaterran   _____

_____ **6.** knab   _____

a.

b.

c.

d.

(continued on next page)

_____ **7.** rat sumuem _____

_____ **8.** tosp cefoif _____

_____ **9.** rkap _____

_____ **10.** rewolf posh _____

_____ **11.** myg _____

_____ **12.** tiploash _____

e.

f.

g.

h.

i.

j.

k.

l.

2 PREPOSITIONS OF PLACE

Look at the map. Read the sentences. Write **T** *or* **F**.

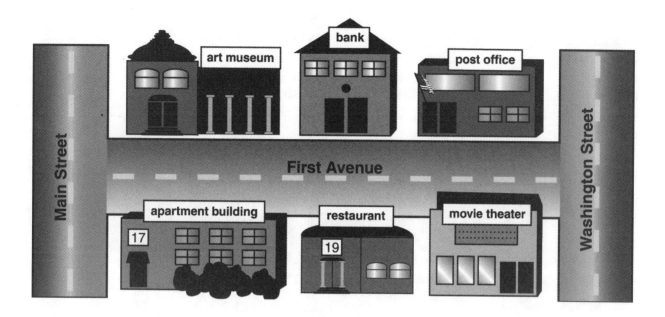

__F__ **1.** The movie theater is across from the restaurant.

__T__ **2.** The post office is across from the movie theater.

_____ **3.** The bank is between the post office and the art museum.

_____ **4.** The apartment building is between the restaurant and the movie theater.

_____ **5.** The art museum is next to the post office.

_____ **6.** The restaurant is on Washington Street.

_____ **7.** The apartment building is at number 17 First Avenue.

_____ **8.** The art museum is across from the apartment building.

3 PREPOSITIONS OF PLACE

Read the description. Write the places on the map.

The bank is at the corner of Tenth Street and West Avenue. It's next to the post office. The movie theater is at the corner of Ninth Street and East Avenue. The art museum is between the movie theater and the Chinese restaurant. The park is across from the restaurant and the art museum. The apartment building is across from the post office. It's between the supermarket and the library. The supermarket is across from the bank.

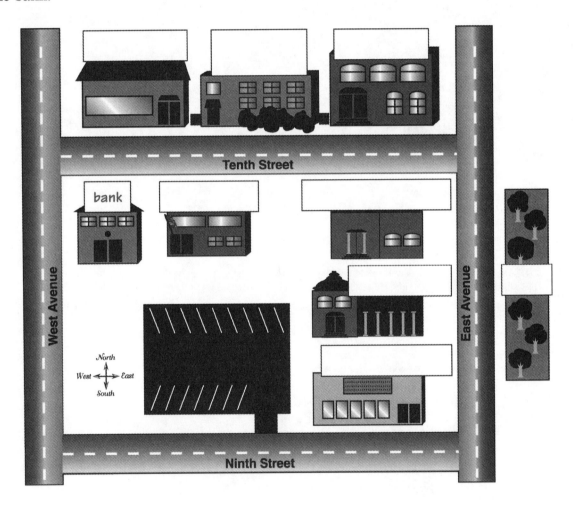

④ THE PRESENT OF *BE*: QUESTIONS WITH *WHERE*

Read the answers. Write questions with **where**.

1. ___Where's Ana from?___ Ana? She's from Brazil.

2. _____ Mr. and Mrs. Lin? They're from Australia.

3. _____ The doctors? They're from Mexico.

4. _____ Paul? He's from Australia.

5. _____ I'm from the United States.

⑤ ORDINAL NUMBERS

Write the words for the numbers.

1. 4th ___fourth___

2. 7th _____

3. 3rd _____

4. 10th _____

⑥ ORDINAL NUMBERS

Write the numbers for the words.

1. ninth ___9th___

2. third _____

3. first _____

4. second _____

7 ORDINAL NUMBERS

Look at the directory. Answer the questions.

MAIN STREET MEDICAL BUILDING	
	FLOOR
Doctor Bell	5
Doctor Chan	1
Doctor Din	3
Doctor Lugo	4
Doctor Peterson	6
Doctor Shore	2

1. Where's Doctor Bell's office?   It's on the fifth floor. _____

2. Where's Doctor Chan's office? _____

3. Where's Doctor Din's office? _____

4. Where's Doctor Lugo's office? _____

5. Where's Doctor Peterson's office? _____

6. Where's Doctor Shore's office? _____

8 EDITING

Correct the e-mail messages. There are seven mistakes. The first one is corrected for you.

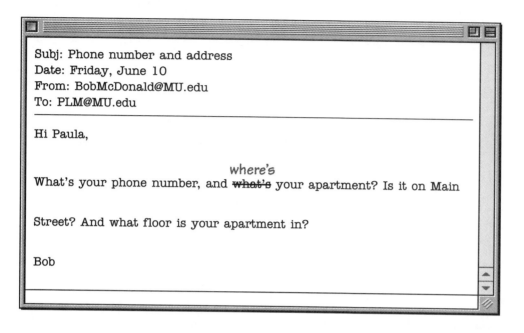

Subj: Phone number and address
Date: Friday, June 10
From: BobMcDonald@MU.edu
To: PLM@MU.edu

Hi Paula,

What's your phone number, and ~~what's~~ your apartment? Is it on Main

Street? And what floor is your apartment in?

Bob

(Above "what's" crossed out: *where's*)

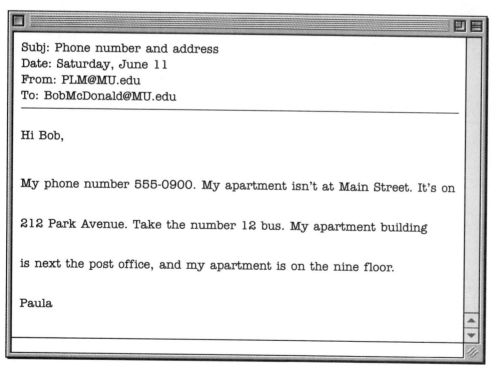

Subj: Phone number and address
Date: Saturday, June 11
From: PLM@MU.edu
To: BobMcDonald@MU.edu

Hi Bob,

My phone number 555-0900. My apartment isn't at Main Street. It's on

212 Park Avenue. Take the number 12 bus. My apartment building

is next the post office, and my apartment is on the nine floor.

Paula

UNIT

7 THE PAST OF *BE*: STATEMENTS, YES / NO QUESTIONS

1 AFFIRMATIVE AND NEGATIVE STATEMENTS WITH THE PAST OF *BE*

Read the sentences. Write **T** *or* **F**.

_____ **1.** I was late for class yesterday.

_____ **2.** I wasn't at the library last night.

_____ **3.** A friend was with me yesterday.

_____ **4.** My teacher wasn't at school yesterday.

_____ **5.** My friends and I were at a movie yesterday.

_____ **6.** My family and I were at home last night.

_____ **7.** My friends were at my home last night.

_____ **8.** My classmates weren't happy in the last English class.

2 AFFIRMATIVE STATEMENTS WITH THE PAST OF *BE*

Write the names of movies.

1. _____Star Wars_____ was exciting.

2. _____ was funny.

3. _____ was scary.

4. _____ was sad.

5. _____ was interesting.

6. The actors in _____ were great.

7. _____ was boring.

8. _____ was awful.

❸ AFFIRMATIVE AND NEGATIVE STATEMENTS WITH THE PAST OF *BE*

Rewrite the sentences. Write about **yesterday**.

1. Ben's at home today.

   Ben was at home yesterday.

2. Kate isn't in class today.

_____

3. I'm happy today.

_____

4. It's cold today.

_____

5. The children are sad today.

_____

6. We aren't noisy today.

_____

7. The streets aren't crowded today.

_____

8. You're hot today.

_____

9. I'm not alone today.

_____

❹ THE PAST OF *BE*: AFFIRMATIVE AND NEGATIVE STATEMENTS

Complete the diary. Use **was**, **wasn't**, **were**, *or* **weren't**.

April 15

Yesterday _____was_____ great. I _____ alone. I _____

1.   2.   3.

with Mark. We _____ at a movie. The movie _____

4.   5.

Frankenstein's Uncle. It _____ really funny.

6.

    Amanda and Josh _____ with me and Mark. They stopped by

7.

my house, but I _____ home. Amanda doesn't know Mark and I

8.

_____ together.

9.

---

❺ YES / NO QUESTIONS AND SHORT ANSWERS WITH THE PAST OF *BE*

Write questions. Then look at the pictures and write short answers.

1. Jeremy / at a movie / last night

Was Jeremy at a movie last night?

No, he wasn't.

2. Tim and Jessica / at a movie / last night

_____

_____

3. Bill and Steve / at a play / yesterday

_____

_____

4. Judy / at a party / yesterday

_____

_____

(continued on next page)

5. Mark / at home / yesterday

_____

_____

6. Mary, Annie, and Ben / at a soccer game / last night

_____

_____

6 EDITING

Correct the conversations. There are seven mistakes. The first one is corrected for you.

1. **A:** ~~They were~~ ^{Were they} at home yesterday?

   B: Yes, they was.

2. **A:** Hi. How it going?

   B: Great.

3. **A:** Were the movie funny yesterday?

   B: No, it isn't.

4. **A:** Where were you the last night?

   B: Was at home.

7 CONVERSATION COMPLETION

Complete the conversation. Use the words in the box. (Don't look at page 44 in your Student Book.)

alone	How's	movie	wasn't
funny	it	~~This~~	were
great	last	was	weren't

KATHY: Hello?

AMANDA: Hi, Kathy. _____This_____ is Amanda.
　　　　　　　　　　　　1.

KATHY: Hi, Amanda. _____ it going?
　　　　　　　　　　　　　2.

AMANDA: Fine. Hey, Josh and I stopped by your house _____ night, but you
　　　　　　　　　　　　　　　　　　　　　　　　　　　　3.

_____ there. Or _____ you asleep?
　　　4.　　　　　　　　**5.**

KATHY: Actually, I _____ home last night. I was at a _____.
　　　　　　　　　　　6.　　　　　　　　　　　　　　　　**7.**

AMANDA: Were you _____?
　　　　　　　　　　8.

KATHY: Uh, no. I _____ with . . . someone. The movie was _____.
　　　　　　　　　9.　　　　　　　　　　　　　　　　　　　**10.**

Really exciting. And _____ too.
　　　　　　　　　　　11.

AMANDA: Really! What movie was _____?
　　　　　　　　　　　　　　　　12.

KATHY: *Frankenstein's Uncle.*

8 THE PAST OF *BE*: *WH-* QUESTIONS

1 *WH-* QUESTIONS WITH THE PAST OF *BE*

Complete the sentences. Circle the correct answers and write them on the lines.

1. _____Who_____ were you with last weekend?

   a. How   **b.** Where   **c.** Who

2. _____ was your weekend?

   a. How   **b.** What   **c.** Where

3. _____ were you yesterday afternoon?

   a. How long   **b.** When   **c.** Where

4. _____ were you there yesterday afternoon?

   a. How long   **b.** Where   **c.** Who

5. _____ did you study English?

   a. What   **b.** When   **c.** Who

6. _____ was at your home last night?

   a. How long   **b.** When   **c.** Who

7. _____ was the weather yesterday?

   a. How   **b.** Where   **c.** When

2 THE PAST OF *BE*: AFFIRMATIVE STATEMENTS

Answer the questions in Exercise 1.

1. I was with my friends.

2. _____

3. _____

4. _____

5. _____

6. _____

7. _____

3 **WH- QUESTIONS WITH THE PAST OF BE**

Look at Jason's postcard. Write Mark's questions.

```
                                              July 4

  Hi everyone,

      It's great here in San Francisco. I'm here on
  vacation for five days with my brother and sister. The
  weather isn't great. It's cool and rainy, but we're
  having fun. See you next week.

                            Jason
```

```
  Jet Travel Books
  111 Washington Ave.
  Seattle, WA 98101
```

MARK: ___When was your vacation?_____
1.

JASON: Last week.

MARK: _____
2.

JASON: It was great.

MARK: _____
3.

JASON: In San Francisco.

MARK: _____
4.

JASON: My brother and sister.

MARK: _____
5.

JASON: Five days.

MARK: _____
6.

JASON: It was cool and rainy.

4 **WORDS AND EXPRESSIONS**

Look at the weather information. Answer the questions.

YESTERDAY'S WEATHER			
City	**°F**	**°C**	**Conditions**
London	45	7	r
Mexico City	98	37	r
New York	20	−5	s
Quebec	−2	−20	c
Sydney	80	28	s
Tokyo	60	14	w
c = cloudy r = rainy s = sunny w = windy			

1. How was the weather in London yesterday?

   It was cool and rainy.

2. How was the weather in Mexico City yesterday?

3. How was the weather in New York yesterday?

4. How was the weather in Quebec yesterday?

5. How was the weather in Sydney yesterday?

6. How was the weather in Tokyo yesterday?

5 EDITING

Correct the conversations. There is one mistake in each conversation.

1. **A:** Where ~~you were~~ ^{were you} last night?

   B: I was at a soccer game.

2. **A:** Who were the students?

   B: They were with their teacher.

3. **A:** How long class?

   B: Two hours.

4. **A:** How was the weather?

   B: Was sunny and warm.

5. **A:** When was they here?

   B: Yesterday.

6. **A:** Who movie was it?

   B: *Star Wars*.

6 CONVERSATION COMPLETION

Complete the conversation. Use the words in the box. (Don't look at page 50 in your Student Book.)

cool	long	was	Who
guide	Remember	weather	wonderful
last	~~vacation~~	Were	you

JASON: Hi, Mark. Welcome back. How was your _____vacation_____?
1.

MARK: Great.

JASON: You look good. Where were _____?
2.

MARK: In Spain.

JASON: Nice. How _____ were you there?
3.

MARK: Ten days. Ten _____ days.
4.

JASON: How was the _____?
5.

MARK: Hot and sunny. But it was _____ at the beach.
6.

JASON: _____ you on a tour?
7.

MARK: No, but I _____ with a guide.
8.

JASON: A guide? _____ was your guide?
9.

MARK: _____ Kathy? At Amanda's wedding? The travel agent?
10.

JASON: Sure. She was your _____?
11.

MARK: Yes. She was in Barcelona _____ week.
12.

JASON: You lucky man!

THE PRESENT PROGRESSIVE: STATEMENTS

1 AFFIRMATIVE STATEMENTS WITH THE PRESENT PROGRESSIVE

Match the sentences.

__e__ 1. Mary is at the library.

____ 2. The little boy is in his bedroom.

____ 3. My father's in the kitchen.

____ 4. Mark and Amanda are at a restaurant.

____ 5. Judy's in her office.

____ 6. The students are in the classroom.

____ 7. The boys are at the park.

____ 8. My grandmother's in the hospital.

a. They're playing soccer.

b. She's talking to her doctor.

c. They're writing sentences.

d. He's sleeping.

e. She's reading a book.

f. He's cooking.

g. They're eating.

h. She's working at her computer.

2 BASE FORM AND VERB + –ING

Complete the chart. Use the –ing *form of the verbs.*

Base Form	Base Form + –ing	Base Form	Base Form + –ing
1. ask	asking	7. look	_____
2. close	_____	8. listen	_____
3. do	_____	9. move	_____
4. dream	_____	10. open	_____
5. enjoy	_____	11. run	_____
6. fix	_____	12. shine	_____

3 AFFIRMATIVE AND NEGATIVE STATEMENTS WITH THE PRESENT PROGRESSIVE

Look at the pictures. Write affirmative and negative sentences in the present progressive.

1. Jeremy / listen to music. He / play a computer game.

  Jeremy's listening to music. He isn't playing a computer game.

2. Tim and Jessica / fix their car. They / watch a movie.

  Tim and Jessica aren't fixing their car. They're watching a movie.

3. Tim / drink. He / eat.

  _____

4. Judy / read. She / talk.

  _____

5. Bill and Steve / listen. They / talk.

  _____

6. The athletes / play basketball. They / play soccer.

  _____

7. Mary, Annie, and Ben / sit in the park. They / sit in the living room.

  _____

4 AFFIRMATIVE AND NEGATIVE STATEMENTS WITH THE PRESENT PROGRESSIVE

Write true sentences about yourself.

1. I / wear / pants / right now

    I'm wearing pants right now. (OR: I'm not wearing pants right now.)

2. I / wear / glasses / right now

    _____

3. I / listen / to music / right now

    _____

4. I / sit / in my bedroom / right now

    _____

5. I / eat / right now

    _____

6. I / sit / with my friend / right now

    _____

7. I / drink / water / right now

    _____

8. I / look / at a computer / right now

    _____

⑤ EDITING

Correct the postcard. There are eight mistakes. The first one is corrected for you.

> It's
> Hello from Seattle. ꟷ raining right now, but
>
> we have fun. Jenny and I are sit in a restaurant. I
>
> eating lunch. The food here in Seattle is good.
>
> Jenny no is eating. She drink coffee. We aren't talk.
>
> Jenny's read the newspaper. I hope you're fine.
>
> Love,
>
> Amy

⑥ CONVERSATION COMPLETION

Complete the conversation. Use the words in the box. (Don't look at pages 58–59 in your Student Book.)

are	I'm	not	They're
fun	is	She	was
I	~~kidding~~	She's	wearing

TIM: Those pictures are from the company picnic.

AL: That's a funny picture. Who's that man?

TIM: It's me.

AL: You're ____kidding____.
     1.

TIM: No. Really! _____ not wearing my glasses.
          2.

AL: Oh. Well, what _____ you doing?
                3.

TIM: My assistant and _____ are playing Frisbee.
                      4.

AL: You're _____ a funny hat.
          5.

TIM: Yeah. It's not my hat. The sun was very hot.

AL: Who are the other people?

TIM: That's our vice president. He's barbecuing chicken.

And our president _____ talking to our
                                6.

new salespeople. _____ all listening
                       7.

carefully. She's the boss.

AL: Where _____ this picnic?
                    8.

TIM: In West Park. It's a great place for a company

picnic.

AL: It looks like _____.
                          9.

TIM: It was . . . Well, it was fun for everyone but Sabrina.

Sabrina's our receptionist. Look at this picture.

She's _____ enjoying the picnic.
              10.

_____ hates picnics, and she hates hot
        11.

weather. _____ dreaming about her cool office.
                 12.

THE PRESENT PROGRESSIVE:
YES / NO QUESTIONS

1 SHORT ANSWERS WITH THE PRESENT PROGRESSIVE

Answer the questions. Write true short answers.

1. Are you doing your homework? _____ Yes, I am. (OR: No, I'm not.) _____

2. Is it raining? _____

3. Are you listening to music? _____

4. Is your teacher talking to you? _____

5. Are your friends doing their homework with you? _____

6. Are you having fun? _____

7. Are you working hard? _____

8. Is the sun shining? _____

2 YES / NO QUESTIONS WITH THE PRESENT PROGRESSIVE

Write yes / no questions. Use the words in parentheses.

1. She's reading. (a book?) _____ Is she reading a book? _____

2. He's sleeping. (in his bedroom?) _____

3. They're writing. (a letter?) _____

4. Ben's doing his homework. (alone?) _____

5. I'm talking. (to your boss?) _____

6. Kelly's daydreaming. (about her vacation?) _____

7. The kids are cleaning. (the bathroom?) _____

8. We're baking. (cookies?) _____

③ YES / NO QUESTIONS AND SHORT ANSWERS WITH THE PRESENT PROGRESSIVE

Write questions. Then look at the picture and write short answers.

1. Jessica / cook chicken

Is Jessica cooking chicken?   Yes, she is.

2. Jessica / wear a hat

Is Jessica wearing a hat?   No, she isn't.

3. Jessica and Tim / eat at a restaurant

4. the cat / wear a hat

5. Ben and Annie / play cards

6. Jeremy / play a computer game

7. Tim / write a letter

8. the cat / sit on the chair

9. the cat / babysit

4 STATEMENTS AND *YES / NO* QUESTIONS WITH THE PRESENT PROGRESSIVE

Complete the conversation. Write statements and yes / no *questions in the present progressive. Use the words in parentheses.*

GAIL: ____Is your mother baking____?
1. (your mother / bake)

ANNIE: No, that's my brother. _____ cookies.
2. (he / make)

GAIL: _____ in the dining room?
3. (your parents / eat)

ANNIE: No, that's Kelly, the babysitter. _____ dinner at a
4. (my parents / have)

restaurant. It's their anniversary.

GAIL: What about Jeremy? _____?
5. (he / sleep)

ANNIE: No, he isn't. _____ magic tricks.
6. (he / do)

5 EDITING

Correct the conversations. There are ten mistakes. The first one is corrected for you.

1. **A:** Are you ~~sleep~~ sleeping?

   B: No, I not.

2. **A:** The teacher asking a question?

   B: Yes, she's.

3. **A:** Is Mr. Olson work?

   B: No, he isn't. He's eat lunch.

4. **A:** Is babysitting Kelly?

   B: No, she's not. She watching a video with her friend.

5. **A:** Is Tim and his boss wearing suits?

   B: Yes, they're.

6 CONVERSATION COMPLETION

Complete the conversation. Use the words in the box. (Don't look at pages 66–67 in your Student Book.)

anniversary	cool	~~going~~	listening
are	doing	having	See
baking	Everything's	homework	sleeping

KELLY: Hello?

JESSICA: Hi, Kelly. This is Mrs. Olson. How's it

_____going_____? Are the children _____
       1.   **2.**

to you?

KELLY: Oh, yes. _____ great.
                              3.

JESSICA: Good. Is Ben _____ his homework?
                             4.

KELLY: No, not now. He's _____. We're
                             5.

making cookies.

JESSICA: Oh? Well, that's nice. Just remind him about his

_____. What about Annie?
     6.

Is she _____?
            7.

KELLY: No. Her friend Gail is here. The girls

_____ playing. They're _____
     8.   **9.**

fun.

JESSICA: Hmm. Well, I'm sure they're okay. But please go

and check.

KELLY: Sure, Mrs. Olson. Don't worry. Everything's

_____. Enjoy your _____.
   10.   **11.**

JESSICA: Thanks, Kelly. _____ you around eleven.
                            12.

THE PRESENT PROGRESSIVE: *WH-* QUESTIONS

QUESTION WORDS

Write the correct question words. Use **who**, **what**, **where**, **why**,
or **how**.

1. _____Where_____?   **a.** In the park.

2. _____?   **b.** Bill and Steve.

3. _____?   **c.** Soccer.

4. _____?   **d.** At a table.

5. _____?   **e.** Because they're having a picnic.

6. _____?   **f.** Great.

7. _____?   **g.** They're listening to the radio.

8. _____?   **h.** Jeremy is.

9. _____?   **i.** Because he's cooking.

② *WH-* QUESTIONS WITH THE PRESENT PROGRESSIVE

Write questions in the present progressive. Then find an answer for each question in Exercise 1.

Tim is wearing an **apron**.

1. Who / Tim / talk / to

_____Who is Tim talking to?_____   _____Bill and Steve._____

2. Where / Tim / barbecue / hot dogs

_____   _____

3. Why / the Olsons / eat / in the park

_____   _____

4. What / the children / play

_____   _____

5. Where / Jessica / sit

_____   _____

6. Why / Tim / wear / an apron

_____   _____

7. How / the picnic / go

_____   _____

8. Who / play / soccer with the children

_____   _____

9. What / Judy and her friends / do

_____   _____

❸ *WH-* QUESTIONS WITH THE PRESENT PROGRESSIVE

Complete the conversations. Write questions with **where**, **what**, **why**, *or* **who**.

1. A: I'm sitting in the garden.

    B: _____Why are you sitting_____ there?

    A: It's a beautiful day.

2. A: Shh! I'm talking.

    B: _____ to?

    A: My grandfather.

3. A: The children are baking.

    B: _____

    A: Cookies.

4. A: Mrs. Brody isn't watching Ben and Annie.

    B: _____ the kids?

    A: Her granddaughter, Kelly, is.

5. A: Jeremy's studying.

    B: _____

    A: At the library.

❹ EDITING

Correct the conversations. There are eight mistakes. The first one is corrected for you.

1. A: What ~~you are~~ doing? (are you)

    B: My homework.

2. A: What the people watching?

    B: The firefighters.

3. A: Why Mark is wearing a suit?

    B: Because he going to a wedding.

4. A: What's everything going?

    B: Great. We have a lot of fun.

5. **A:** Where Ben and Annie are going?

   B: To their grandmother's house.

6. **A:** Who's Jeremy send an e-mail message to?

   B: A friend from school.

5 CONVERSATION COMPLETION

Complete the conversations. Use the words in the box. (Don't look at page 72 in your Student Book.)

Apple pie with ice cream	I'm	starved	Where's
Broccoli	on	What	Who
~~Dad's~~	out	What's	Why

ANNIE: Hey, Mom. _____Dad's_____ driving down the street.
1.

_____ he going?
2.

JESSICA: To the store.

ANNIE: _____ is he going to the store now?
3.

JESSICA: Because we're _____ of milk.
4.

ANNIE: Oh. _____ for dinner?
5.

JESSICA: Your favorite!

ANNIE: My favorite? Really? What?

JESSICA: _____.
6.

ANNIE: Mom! Come _____! Are you kidding?
7.

JESSICA: Yes, _____ kidding.
8.

[*Later*]

(continued on next page)

JEREMY: Hi, Mom. _____ are you talking to?
9.

JESSICA: Dad. He's at the supermarket.

JEREMY: _____ are you making?
10.

JESSICA: Spaghetti.

JEREMY: With meat sauce?

JESSICA: Yes. Of course with meat sauce.

JEREMY: Mmm. Good deal. I'm _____. What's for
11.

dessert?

JESSICA: _____.
12.

THE SIMPLE PRESENT: STATEMENTS

1 AFFIRMATIVE AND NEGATIVE STATEMENTS WITH THE SIMPLE PRESENT

True or false? Write **T** *or* **F**. *(Look at your Student Book if you need help.)*

__F__ **1.** Jessica has a brother and a sister.

__T__ **2.** Jessica and Tim have three children.

_____ **3.** Steve doesn't have children.

_____ **4.** Mary doesn't live with her children, Jessica and Steve.

_____ **5.** Mary lives with her husband, Bill.

_____ **6.** Steve works at a university.

_____ **7.** Jessica and Tim don't work.

_____ **8.** Jeremy likes computer games.

_____ **9.** Mark doesn't like Kathy.

2 AFFIRMATIVE STATEMENTS WITH THE SIMPLE PRESENT

Complete the sentences. Use the verbs in the box.

act	babysit	play	report	sing	teach	~~write~~

1. Mark is a writer. He ____writes____ travel books.

2. Jessica is a news reporter. She _____ the news.

3. Steve is a teacher. He _____ journalism.

4. Matt Damon and Robin Williams are actors. They _____ in movies.

5. Kelly is a babysitter. She _____ for the Olsons.

6. Céline Dion is a singer. She _____ in French and English.

7. Ronaldo and Mario are soccer players. They _____ soccer.

❸ THE SIMPLE PRESENT: NEGATIVE VERBS

Complete the sentences with negative verbs.

1. We want pizza, but we _____don't want_____ dessert.

2. The restaurant has ice cream, but it _____ apple pie.

3. I speak Spanish, but I _____ Portuguese.

4. Kelly and Ken need a computer, but they _____ a TV.

5. We like coffee, but we _____ tea.

6. My sister wants a dog, but she _____ a cat.

7. You have mistakes in Exercise 1, but you _____ mistakes in Exercise 2.

8. Jack teaches on Mondays and Wednesdays, but he _____ on Tuesdays

or Thursdays.

9. It rains a lot in Seattle, but it _____ a lot in Los Angeles.

❹ AFFIRMATIVE AND NEGATIVE STATEMENTS WITH THE SIMPLE PRESENT

*Look at the pictures. Write true statements about yourself. Use **like**.*

1.

milk

_____I like milk._____

_____

2.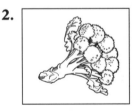

broccoli

_____

_____

3.

spaghetti

_____

_____

4.

apple pie

_____

_____

5.

ice cream

_____

_____

6.

pizza

_____

_____

5 AFFIRMATIVE AND NEGATIVE STATEMENTS WITH THE SIMPLE PRESENT

Write the correct verb forms. Use the verbs in parentheses.

I _____*have*_____ a brother and a sister. My sister and I _____ alike, but my
  1. (have)   **2. (look)**

brother and I _____ alike. My sister and I _____ brown hair and brown
              3. (not look)   **4. (have)**

eyes. My brother _____ black hair and blue eyes. My sister and I both
                   5. (have)

_____. My sister _____ in an office. I _____ in a library. My
  6. (work)   **7. (work)**   **8. (work)**

brother _____. He _____ to school, and on weekends he
        9. (not work)   **10. (go)**

_____ cars. He _____ cars, but he _____ school. At work and
  11. (fix)   **12. (love)**   **13. (not love)**

at school, we _____ English, but we _____ English at home. At home
              14. (speak)   **15. (not speak)**

we _____ Spanish. That's because my parents _____ from the United
  16. (speak)   **17. (not come)**

States. My father _____ from Peru and my mother _____ from Mexico.
                  18. (come)   **19. (come)**

My mother _____ English and Spanish, but my father _____ English.
          20. (speak)   **21. (not speak)**

6 EDITING

*Correct the description of Judy's family. There are ten mistakes. The first one is corrected
for you.*

    My brother, Ken, ~~live~~ *lives* with my parents. They lives in a big house. My father have a new

car. He cleans his car every day. Ken not have a new car. His car is old. It don't run, but he

love it. My mother no love cars. She love her garden. She is work in it every Saturday and

Sunday. I doesn't see my family often, but we talk on the weekend.

7 CONVERSATION COMPLETION

Complete the conversation. Use the words in the box. (Don't look at page 80 in your Student Book.)

doesn't	~~get~~	hair	look
don't	go	likes	sounds
eyes	goes	lives	watch

JUDY: I need more coffee. Can I _____*get*_____ you
1.

some?

MARK: Yes, please.

JUDY: Here you _____.
2.

MARK: Thanks.

JUDY: Oh! New photos?

MARK: Yep . . . Look at this one. This is my brother,

Nick. He _____ in Alaska.
3.

JUDY: You _____ alike.
4.

MARK: I know. We both have blond _____ and
5.

blue _____.
6.

JUDY: And you're both tall.

MARK: But we're different in a lot of ways.

JUDY: How?

MARK: Well, I like people and parties. Nick

_____ computers. I _____ like
7.   8.

computers, and Nick _____ like parties.
9.

JUDY: Oh, really?

MARK: Yeah. And I speak Mandarin. Nick speaks

Spanish. I read newspapers and magazines. Nick

reads novels. I _____ TV almost every
10.

night, but Nick _____ online.
11.

JUDY: Yeah? He _____ interesting.
12.

THE SIMPLE PRESENT: YES / NO QUESTIONS

 1 YES / NO QUESTIONS WITH THE SIMPLE PRESENT

*Are the questions for Annie or for Jessica? Write **A** or **J**.*

- _J_ **1.** Do your children clean their rooms?
- _A_ **2.** Does your father read you a story at night?
- ____ **3.** Does your husband cook?
- ____ **4.** Does your mother drive you to school?
- ____ **5.** Do your parents live with your brother?
- ____ **6.** Do you like school?
- ____ **7.** Do your parents help you with your homework?
- ____ **8.** Do you visit your parents on the weekend?
- ____ **9.** Does your brother teach at a language school or at a university?
- ____ **10.** Do your brothers play games with you?

❷ YES / NO QUESTIONS AND SHORT ANSWERS WITH THE SIMPLE PRESENT

Match the questions and answers.

___d___ **1.** Do you sleep every day?

_____ **2.** Do people in Japan speak Japanese?

_____ **3.** Does it snow in Canada?

_____ **4.** Do you read novels in English?

_____ **5.** Does the sun shine at night?

_____ **6.** Do teachers do homework?

a. No, it doesn't.

b. Yes, it does.

c. No, I don't.

d. Yes, I do.

e. No, they don't.

f. Yes, they do.

❸ SHORT ANSWERS WITH THE SIMPLE PRESENT

Look at the chart. Answer the questions with short answers.

DO THEY LIKE . . . ?	KEN	JUDY	NICK	AMY
CHOCOLATE	yes	yes	no	yes
COMPUTER GAMES	yes	no	yes	yes
HATS	no	no	yes	no
MUSIC	no	yes	yes	yes
NOVELS	yes	no	no	yes

1. Does Ken like chocolate? __Yes, he does.__

2. Does Ken like hats? __No, he doesn't.__

3. Does Amy like hats? _____

4. Do Nick and Judy like novels? _____

5. Does Judy like computer games? _____

6. Do Nick and Amy like computer games? _____

7. Does Judy like chocolate? _____

8. Do you like hats? _____

9. Do you like computer games? _____

4 YES / NO QUESTIONS WITH THE SIMPLE PRESENT

Write yes / no *questions in the simple present tense. Use the words in parentheses.*

1. Jeremy doesn't play baseball. (basketball?)

   _Does he play basketball?_____

2. Jessica doesn't work on Saturday. (on Sunday?)

   _____

3. Mark doesn't speak Spanish. (Japanese?)

   _____

4. Tim and Jessica don't have a dog. (cat?)

   _____

5. Judy doesn't know Amanda. (Kathy?)

   _____

6. Mary and Bill don't need a new clock. (a new radio?)

   _____

7. The school has a library. (gym?)

   _____

8. I don't speak English at home. (Portuguese?)

   _____

5 VERB TENSE REVIEW: PRESENT OF *BE*, PRESENT PROGRESSIVE, SIMPLE PRESENT

Complete the conversations. Use **do**, **does**, **is**, *or* **are**.

1. **A:** _____Is_____ your teacher's name Sara Brody?

   B: No, it isn't.

   A: _____Do_____ you know Sara Brody?

   B: No. Sorry.

(continued on next page)

2. **A:** _____ you married?

   B: Yes. That's my wife next to the door.

   A: _____ you have children?

   B: Yes. We have three—two girls and a boy.

3. **A:** _____ you have homework?

   B: Yeah.

   A: _____ it easy?

   B: Yeah.

4. **A:** Hi. _____ you doing the homework?

   B: Yeah.

   A: _____ you know the answer to question 3?

   B: No. Sorry.

5. **A:** _____ you and your sister look alike?

   B: Not really.

   A: _____ she have blond hair?

   B: No. She has brown hair.

6. **A:** _____ you making coffee?

   B: Yeah. _____ you want some?

   A: Yes, please.

   B: Here you go.

7. **A:** _____ it raining?

   B: Yes.

   A: _____ it rain a lot here?

   B: Yes.

6 STATEMENTS AND *YES / NO* QUESTIONS WITH THE SIMPLE PRESENT

Complete the conversation. Write statements and yes / no *questions in the simple present. Use the words in parentheses.*

ANNIE: _____We want_____ a gift for our brother.
1. (we / want)

SALESPERSON: _____ scarves?
2. (he / like)

BEN: No, he doesn't.

SALESPERSON: _____ hats?
3. (your brother / wear)

ANNIE: Yeah. _____ a good idea.
4. (that / be)

SALESPERSON: What about color? _____ purple?
5. (you / like)

ANNIE: Yeah. _____ purple.
6. (I / love)

BEN: But _____ purple.
7. (Jeremy / not like)

_____ a blue hat?
8. (you / have)

_____ blue hats.
9. (Jeremy / love)

7 EDITING

Correct the conversations. There are eight mistakes. The first one is corrected for you.

1. **A:** ~~You~~ Do you know Jeremy?

   B: No. Who is he?

2. **A:** Does your grandmother knits?

   B: Yes, she is.

3. **A:** Your three friends do play basketball?

   B: One friend play basketball. The other two play soccer.

4. **A:** *Focus on Grammar* have a lot of grammar practice?

   B: Yes, it has.

5. **A:** Do you and the other students like this book?

   B: No, we don't like.

THE SIMPLE PRESENT: *WH-* QUESTIONS

1 *WH-* QUESTIONS WITH THE SIMPLE PRESENT

Match the questions and answers.

__d__ **1.** What time do you wake up?   **a.** At 8:00 and 10:30.

____ **2.** Where do you catch the bus?   **b.** I go home.

____ **3.** How do you know Amanda?   **c.** On Sundays.

____ **4.** Who knows the answer?   **d.** At about 6:00 A.M.

____ **5.** What do you do after class?   **e.** I do.

____ **6.** Why do you take the bus to work?   **f.** She's my cousin.

____ **7.** What time does the movie start?   **g.** On Main Street.

____ **8.** When does he visit his grandparents?   **h.** I don't have a car.

2 *WH-* QUESTIONS WITH THE SIMPLE PRESENT

Complete the questions.

1. A: I go to school.

   B: Where _____ *do you go to school* _____?

2. A: I don't go to school alone.

   B: Who _____ with you?

3. A: I don't get to school by bus.

   B: How _____?

4. A: We do different things in school.

   B: What _____?

5. A: My brother goes to school early.

   B: Why _____?

6. A: Ms. Thomas goes home for lunch.

    B: What time _____?

7. A: We play games in class.

    B: When _____?

3 TELLING TIME

It's seven o'clock.
It's seven.

It's five after seven.

It's a quarter to eight.

It's a quarter after seven.

It's twenty-five to eight.

It's half past seven.
It's seven-thirty.

Write the times.

1. 7:10 _____ It's ten after seven. _____

2. 7:20 _____

3. 7:25 _____

4. 7:40 _____

5. 7:50 _____

6. 7:55 _____

7. 11:00 _____

8. 1:30 _____

9. 2:15 _____

10. 6:45 _____

11. 10:25 _____

12. 3:35 _____

4 *WH-* QUESTIONS WITH THE SIMPLE PRESENT

Complete the conversations. Write questions. Use **what, what time, where, who,** *or* **why**.

1. **A:** ___What time do you wake up?___

   B: I wake up at 7:30.

2. **A:** _____

   B: That store? It sells CDs and cassettes.

3. **A:** _____

   B: Because I like to knit sweaters. It's my hobby.

4. **A:** _____

   B: Colors? I like blue and purple.

5. **A:** _____

   B: I like chocolate a lot, but my sister doesn't.

6. **A:** _____

   B: Two of my cousins live here. My other cousins live in different cities.

7. **A:** _____

   B: My father? He's a writer.

5 EDITING

Correct the conversation. There are eight mistakes. The first two are corrected for you.

YUKO: What time ∧ English class ~~starts~~?
(does)   (start)

OMAR: At 1:00.

YUKO: What time class finish?

OMAR: At 2:30.

YUKO: What means *dislike*?

OMAR: It means "not like."

YUKO: How you say this word?

OMAR: I don't know.

YUKO: Do the teacher teach every day?

OMAR: No. She doesn't teach on Friday.

YUKO: What have we for homework?

OMAR: Page 97.

YUKO: Why does Elena know all the answers?

OMAR: She study a lot.

6 CONVERSATION COMPLETION

Complete the conversation. Use the words in the box. (Don't look at page 94 in your Student Book.)

cooking	~~how~~	quarter	time
early	late	Talking	What
else	mean	ticket agent	Where

KATHY: So . . . ____how____ do you like
1.
married life?

AMANDA: It's wonderful! But . . . really different.

KATHY: What do you _____?
2.

AMANDA: Well, Josh and I are opposites. For one

thing, he goes to bed _____,
3.
and I stay up late.

KATHY: What _____ does he go to
4.
bed?

AMANDA: Eight-thirty or a _____ to
5.
nine. He starts work at 6:00 A.M.

KATHY: _____ does he work?
6.

AMANDA: At the airport.

KATHY: Oh, no wonder. What does he do?

(continued on next page)

AMANDA: He's a _____.
7.

KATHY: How _____ do *you* stay up?
8.

AMANDA: At least until midnight.

KATHY: Yeah. That *is* different. What _____?
9.

AMANDA: Well, he loves _____, and I hate it. He doesn't like most sports, and I
10.

love them.

KATHY: Really? That's too bad. _____ do you have in common?
11.

AMANDA: _____. We talk for hours and hours. About everything.
12.

KATHY: That's good.

THE SIMPLE PRESENT: *BE* AND *HAVE*

1 AFFIRMATIVE SIMPLE PRESENT STATEMENTS WITH *BE* AND *HAVE*

Look at the pictures. Write **Tom**, **Sue**, *or* **Vic** *next to the sentences.*

Tom   **Sue**   **Vic**

Sue	**1.** This person is thin.
_____	**2.** This person is a child.
_____	**3.** This person is tall.
_____	**4.** This person is about twenty-four years old.
_____	**5.** This person is twelve years old.
_____	**6.** This person has curly gray hair.
_____	**7.** This person is an athlete.
_____	**8.** This person is heavy.
_____	**9.** This person has dark brown hair.
_____	**10.** This person is a musician.

❷ SIMPLE PRESENT STATEMENTS WITH *BE* AND *HAVE*

Complete the sentences about yourself. Use **'m**, **'m not**, **have**, *or* **don't have**.

1. I _____ divorced.

2. I _____ one brother and one sister.

3. I _____ nineteen years old.

4. I _____ hazel eyes.

5. I _____ curly hair.

6. I _____ a university student.

7. I _____ a job.

8. I _____ medium height.

9. I _____ from Mexico.

10. I _____ light brown hair.

❸ SIMPLE PRESENT STATEMENTS WITH *BE* AND *HAVE*

Complete the description. Use the correct forms of **be** *or* **have**.

These ____*are*____ pictures of Bono and his band. The name of the band
   1.
_____ U2. Bono _____ the singer in the band.
   2.   3.
Bono _____ his real name. His real name _____ Paul Hewson.
          4.   5.
He _____ from Dublin, Ireland. He _____ one brother, but he
       6.   7.
_____ any sisters.
   8.

He _____ married to Alison Stewart. They _____ four children—
         9.   **10.**
two daughters and two sons. They _____ a home in Dublin. Their children's
                                         11.
names _____ Jordan, Memphis Eve, Elijah, and John Abraham.
         12.

4 SIMPLE PRESENT QUESTIONS WITH *BE* AND *HAVE*

Write questions about Bono. Use the words in parentheses and the correct forms of
be *or* **have**.

1. (Who / the man in the pictures / ?) __Who's the man in the pictures?_____

2. (Bono / in a band / ?) __Is Bono in a band?_____

3. (What / the name of Bono's band / ?) _____

4. (Bono / a violinist / ?) _____

5. (What / Bono's real name / ?) _____

6. (Where / he from / ?) _____

7. (he / any brothers or sisters / ?) _____

8. (he / married / ?) _____

9. (they / children / ?) _____

10. (Where / they / a home / ?) _____

5 EDITING

Correct the conversation. There are eight mistakes. The first one is corrected for you.

                 What's
A: ~~What~~ your name?

B: Alice.

A: How old have you?

B: I have twenty-four.

A: You have a big family?

B: Yes, I do. I have three sisters and four brothers.

A: Where do you live?

B: My home near here. It's on Center Street.

(continued on next page)

A: Is big?

B: No. It small. I live alone. My family lives in another city.

A: Have you a job?

B: No. I study at a university.

---

6 **CONVERSATION COMPLETION**

Complete the conversation. Use the words in the box. (Don't look at pages 100–101 in your Student Book.)

does	He	isn't	think
has	He's	like	was
have	is	That's	~~Where~~

JUDY: Look!

MARK: ___Where___?
1.

JUDY: There. On the second floor in the window . . . Never mind. The boy

_____ there now.
2.

MARK: What boy?

JUDY: I see a young boy in that window every day. He plays the violin.

MARK: Hmm. How old _____ he?
3.

JUDY: About eight or nine.

MARK: What does he look _____?
4.

JUDY: _____ a good-looking boy. He _____ dark hair and big brown
                5.   6.

eyes. _____ has a scar on his right cheek.
          7.

MARK: Does he _____ long arms and legs and curly hair?
                        8.

JUDY: Yes, he _____.
                      9.

MARK: Is his hair a little long?

JUDY: I _____ so. Why?
              10.

MARK: He's famous. He _____ on the news just last night.
                              11.

JUDY: Really?

MARK: Yes. And look at the paper. He's here too.

JUDY: Well, look at that! _____ the boy.
                                  12.

ADVERBS OF FREQUENCY

① ADVERBS OF FREQUENCY WITH *BE* AND OTHER VERBS

True or false? Write **T** *or* **F**.

_____ **1.** I always do my homework.

_____ **2.** I never get up early.

_____ **3.** I sometimes go to bed at 9:00.

_____ **4.** I'm usually tired in class.

_____ **5.** I often have fun in class.

_____ **6.** I'm not usually hungry in the morning.

_____ **7.** I rarely exercise in the morning.

_____ **8.** I don't always make dinner.

② WORD ORDER WITH ADVERBS OF FREQUENCY

Put the words in the correct order. Write sentences.

1. late / sleep / never / I / .

   I never sleep late.

2. does / Steve / exercise / often / not / .

_____

3. rarely / a / Bill / restaurant / eats / at / .

_____

4. here / It / snows / sometimes / .

_____

5. Mary / not / usually / busy / is / .

_____

6. Cairo / often / is / It / hot / in / .

_____

❸ ADVERBS OF FREQUENCY

Rewrite the sentences. Replace the underlined words. Use **always**, **often**, **sometimes**, **rarely**, *or* **never**.

1. Omar is happy <u>every day</u>.

    Omar is always happy.

2. I <u>don't</u> drink coffee.

    I never drink coffee.

3. I play soccer <u>one or two times a month</u>.

4. Jessica cooks dinner <u>two or three times a week</u>.

5. I am late for class <u>one or two times a year</u>.

6. The food at that restaurant is <u>not</u> good.

7. Annie and Ben start school at 8:30 <u>every day</u>.

8. Josh goes to the gym <u>three times a week</u>.

9. The park is crowded <u>on Sundays</u>.

10. Robert goes to the movies <u>one time a year</u>.

4 QUESTIONS WITH *EVER* AND *HOW OFTEN*

Complete the conversations. Write questions. Use **ever** *or* **how often**.

1. A: ___How often do you go dancing?___

   B: Go dancing? I never go dancing.

2. A: ___Do you ever go dancing?___

   B: Yes, I do. I go dancing three or four times a year.

3. A: _____

   B: No, they don't. My children never stay home alone.

4. A: _____

   B: The radio? I listen to the radio every day.

5. A: _____

   B: No, never. I never smoke.

6. A: _____

   B: Tim? He cooks dinner one or two times a week.

7. A: _____

   B: No. I'm not usually busy on the weekend.

5 EDITING

Correct the paragraph. There are six mistakes. The first one is corrected for you.

                         am usually
    Here is my schedule. I ~~usually am~~ busy on Monday evenings. I go often to the gym,

or I play basketball. (Do ever you play basketball?) On Fridays always I exercise too. I go

dancing! On Wednesdays and Thursdays I sometimes work late, but I'm often free on

Tuesdays. I finish work usually at 5:30. Do you want to meet at Vincenzo's Italian

Restaurant at 6:30? The food there is good always.

6 CONVERSATION COMPLETION

Complete the conversation. Use the words in the box. (Don't look at page 106 in your Student Book.)

always	enough	hurry	sleep
breakfast	ever	~~matter~~	Sometimes
energy	hours	often	times

JOSH: What's the <u>matter</u> , Steve? You look
1.
really tired.

STEVE: I *am* tired. I never have enough

_____ anymore.
2.

JOSH: That's too bad. Any idea why?

STEVE: Well, maybe I'm not getting enough

_____ .
3.

JOSH: How much are you getting?

STEVE: Oh, about six _____ a night.
4.

JOSH: What time do you go to bed?

STEVE: Hmm . . . I usually stay up till 1:00. And I get up at 7:00.

JOSH: Do you _____ sleep late?
5.

STEVE: _____—on the weekend.
6.

JOSH: What about food? Do you eat three meals a day? Breakfast, lunch, and dinner?

STEVE: Well . . . not really. I'm usually in a _____ in the morning. So I skip
7.

_____ .
8.

JOSH: Not good, my friend. What about lunch and dinner?

STEVE: I _____ have a good dinner. But lunch . . . well, I usually go to a fast-
9.
food place near the university.

JOSH: Hmm. Not _____ sleep. No breakfast. Fast food for lunch. You're living
10.
dangerously.

STEVE: Maybe. But I have one good habit. I exercise.

JOSH: Great. How _____?
11.

STEVE: Two or three _____ a year.
12.

UNIT

17 POSSESSIVE NOUNS; *THIS / THAT / THESE / THOSE*

1 THIS / THAT / THESE / THOSE

What are the people saying? Write questions with **what**. *Use* **this, that, these,** *or* **those**.

1.

2.

3.

4.

❷ VOCABULARY

Unscramble the words. Then match the words with the pictures in Exercise 1.

1. etahcre   __teacher__   Picture __3__

2. dsrbi   _____   Picture ____

3. earpp gba   _____   Picture ____

4. spursneeds   _____   Picture ____

❸ POSSESSIVE NOUNS

Look at the picture. Complete the sentences.

Meg   Juan   Renee   Amy   Ari

1. ____Ari's____ hat is black.

2. _____ hair is blond.

3. _____ vest is white.

4. _____ vest is black.

5. _____ sunglasses are nice.

❹ POSSESSIVE NOUNS

Correct the sentences. Add **'s** *or* **'** *where necessary. The first one is done for you.*

1. Jessica^{'s} house is big.

2. His parents names are Jessica and Tim.

3. Steve apartment is in Seattle.

4. The students chairs are between the board and the window.

5. The teacher desk is near the door.

(continued on next page)

6. Our daughters husbands are very nice.

7. The children room is on the second floor.

8. My friend grandchildren visit her often.

5 POSSESSIVE 'S OR CONTRACTION?

Rewrite the sentences where possible.

1. Jack's wearing black shoes.

    Jack is wearing black shoes.

2. Who's wearing Mara's jacket?

3. That's not Judy's backpack.

4. The baby's not sleeping.

5. What's Steve's last name?

6. Amanda's here.

7. Where's the car?

6 EDITING

Correct the conversations. There are six mistakes. The first one is corrected for you.

1. A: Does my ~~mother~~ jacket look good on me?
           mother's

    B: Hmm. I'm not sure.

2. A: The women restroom is over there.

    B: Thanks.

(continued on next page)

3. A: Who's this over there?

    B: That's Ken.

4. A: Does Ken usually wear ties?

    B: No. He's wearing his brother tie. And this isn't Ken's sports jacket either.

5. A: Those earrings look really good on Judy.

    B: Yeah. I like Rose earrings too.

7 CONVERSATION COMPLETION

Complete the conversation. Use the words in the box. (Don't look at page 114 in your Student Book.)

brother's	Steve's	that	this
Kathy's	parents	these	those
~~occasion~~	parents'	They're	yours

JUDY: Mark, you look sharp! What's the ___*occasion*___?
                                            1.

MARK: Dinner—with Kathy and her _____. It's
                                        2.

        her _____ anniversary. Is the jacket
                    3.

        okay?

JUDY: It's fine.

MARK: It's my _____.
                 4.

JUDY: I like _____ shoes.
               5.

MARK: _____ my roommate's. How
          6.

        about _____ tie? Does it match
                7.

        _____ suspenders?
        8.

JUDY: It's a perfect match.

MARK: The tie is _____. The suspenders are his
                     9.

        too.

JUDY: Is *anything* _____?
                  10.

MARK: Sure. This new goatee. It's all mine.

(continued on next page)

JUDY: Oh. I see. Well, _____ goatee makes you look like a doctor.
11.

MARK: Good. Now I need to remember—_____ mom is Liz, and her dad is
12.

Russ, not Ross. When I'm nervous, I forget names.

JUDY: Mark, you look wonderful. Don't be nervous. And just don't call Kathy's dad Rose.

COUNT AND NON-COUNT NOUNS:
SOME AND ANY

1 COUNT AND NON-COUNT NOUNS

Write **a**, **an**, *or* **some** *before each word.*

_a_	**1.** bagel		_____	**13.** olive
some	**2.** bread		_____	**14.** orange
_____	**3.** banana		_____	**15.** peach
_____	**4.** cereal		_____	**16.** peanut butter
_____	**5.** chip		_____	**17.** rice
_____	**6.** coffee		_____	**18.** sandwich
_____	**7.** egg		_____	**19.** soda
_____	**8.** fruit		_____	**20.** spaghetti
_____	**9.** hamburger		_____	**21.** strawberry
_____	**10.** ice cream		_____	**22.** toast
_____	**11.** juice		_____	**23.** water
_____	**12.** milk		_____	**24.** yogurt

2 SOME AND ANY

Rewrite the sentences with plural nouns. Use **some** *or* **any**.

1. Give me a bagel, please.

   Give me some bagels, please.

2. I don't want a banana.

   I don't want any bananas.

3. I don't have an orange.

   _____

4. Eat an egg.

   _____

(continued on next page)

5. We need a sandwich.

_____

6. She wants an olive.

_____

7. Do you need a strawberry?

_____

3 QUANTIFIERS WITH NON-COUNT NOUNS

Complete the sentences. Use the words in the box.

bag	bottle	bowl	cup	glass	slice

1. I want a _____bottle_____ of water.

_____cup_____

_____glass_____

2. I have a _____ of iced tea.

_____

3. Here is a _____ of coffee.

_____

4. I don't want a _____ of bread.

5. Do you want a _____ of rice?

_____

_____

4 VERB AGREEMENT WITH COUNT AND NON-COUNT NOUNS

*Complete the sentences. Use **is** or **are**.*

1. Here _____are_____ some bagels.

2. Here _____is_____ some tea.

3. Some fruit _____ on the table.

4. This _____ juice.

5. Eggs _____ good for you.

6. The ice cream _____ delicious.

7. Olives _____ usually black, brown, or green.

8. The food at that restaurant _____ good.

5 COUNT AND NON-COUNT NOUNS

Complete the sentences. Use **a, an, any,** *or* **some**.

1. I don't have _____*any*_____ sisters or brothers.

2. I'm writing _____*an*_____ e-mail message.

3. Do you have _____ questions?

4. I have _____ question.

5. I need _____ answer to this question.

6. I know _____ people from Canada.

7. I don't have _____ American friends.

8. We have _____ apartment on Main Street.

9. Do you like _____ green vegetables?

10. We want _____ tea.

11. I don't want _____ ice cream.

12. Please give me _____ bananas.

6 EDITING

Correct the conversation. There are seven mistakes. The first one is corrected for you.

JOSH: Waiter? Excuse me. Can I have ~~some~~ *a* glass of water, please?

WAITER: Sure. Ma'am, do you want a water?

JUDY: Yes, thank you.

[*Minutes later*]

WAITER: Here is your water. What would you like to eat?

JUDY: I'd like some sandwich and some iced tea. Oh, and some bowl of chocolate ice cream too.

WAITER: And you, sir?

JOSH: Tell me. Are the spaghetti here good?

(continued on next page)

WAITER: Yes, delicious.

JOSH: Okay. I'd like any spaghetti.

WAITER: And what about something to drink?

JOSH: I just want these water.

---

7 CONVERSATION COMPLETION

Complete the conversations. Use the words in the box. (Don't look at page 120 in your Student Book.)

~~a~~	at	fruit	on
all	bowl	glass	some
an	cup	in	strawberries

JESSICA: Hello, everyone. This morning we're interviewing people about their eating habits. Here's our first person. Sir, do you eat breakfast?

MAN: Yes, I do.

JESSICA: What do you have?

MAN: I have _____*a*_____ bagel and a _____
　　　　　　　　1.　　　　　　　　　　　　　2.
of coffee.

JESSICA: That's _____?
　　　　　　　　　3.

MAN: Yes. I'm always _____ a hurry. 'Bye!
　　　　　　　　　　　　　4.

JESSICA: Okay. Thanks. 'Bye.

JESSICA: Now, here's our next person. Ma'am, what do you have for breakfast?

WOMAN 1: I never eat breakfast.

JESSICA: Nothing _____ all?
　　　　　　　　　　　5.

WOMAN 1: No. I'm _____ a diet.
　　　　　　　　　　6.

JESSICA: Okay. Thank you . . .

JESSICA: And what about you, ma'am? What do you have for

breakfast?

WOMAN 2: Oh, I usually have a _____ of cereal and
                                        7.

_____ yogurt with _____—a
          8.   9.

banana, a peach or _____ orange, or
                              10.

some _____. And I have a
              11

_____ of juice.
          12.

JESSICA: Hmm. That sounds healthy.

A / An and *The*; *One* / *Ones*

① ONE / ONES

Match the sentences.

___f___ **1.** I like the blue blazer.

_____ **2.** Here are your new suspenders.

_____ **3.** Do you like the stores
   on Main Street?

_____ **4.** I like the black pants.

_____ **5.** This is your new office.

_____ **6.** Do you go to the Italian
   restaurant on Park Street?

a. No, I don't like that one.

b. No, I like the ones on
   First Street.

c. I like the brown ones.

d. I like the old one.

e. I want the old ones.

f. Really? I like the red one.

② ONE / ONES

Look at the pictures. Answer the questions. Use **one** *or* **ones**.

1. Do you like the cheap car or the expensive car?

   I like the expensive one. (OR: I like the cheap one.)

2. Do you like the formal shoes or the casual shoes?

_____

3. Do you like the old cell phone or the new cell phone?

_____

 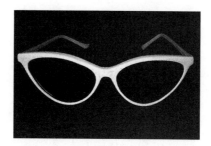

4. Do you like the black sunglasses or the white sunglasses?

_____

3 THE DEFINITE ARTICLE (*THE*)

*Complete the conversations. Use **the** where necessary.*

1. **A:** Does Tim like _____ —_____ hats?

   B: No, he never wears them.

2. **A:** I like _____ *the* _____ hats in that store.

   B: Yeah, they're nice.

3. **A:** What do we need?

   B: We need _____ bananas.

4. **A:** Do you ever eat at Tom's Restaurant?

   B: No, I don't like _____ hamburgers there.

5. **A:** Where's Annie?

   B: In _____ kitchen.

6. **A:** Open _____ windows, please.

   B: Okay.

7. **A:** Do you ever eat _____ eggs for breakfast?

   B: No, never.

8. **A:** How do _____ shoes feel?

   B: Great. They're really comfortable.

9. **A:** Have some strawberries.

   B: I don't like _____ strawberries.

10. **A:** These pants are for Mary.

    B: But she doesn't wear _____ pants.

4 A / AN AND *THE*

Complete the paragraphs. Use **a**, **an**, *or* **the** *where necessary.*

I shop at Clothes For You. It's _____*a*_____ nice store. It always has _____–_____
1.   2.
clothes in my size. It has _____ clothes for _____ men and
                          3.   4.
_____ women. _____ clothes there are always stylish and not very
5.   6.
expensive.

I go to Nice Feet for _____ shoes. _____ shoes there are a little
                      7.   8.
expensive, but they're always comfortable. It's _____ big store, and it's usually
                                                9.
busy. I know _____ clerk there. I don't know his name, but he's the only clerk
             10.
there with _____ goatee. He also always wears _____ orange tie.
           11.   12.

5 EDITING

Correct the conversations. There are eight mistakes. The first one is corrected for you.

1. **A:** Try on the green jacket.

   B: But I prefer the brown. ^*one*

2. **A:** What's your favorite food?

   B: I like the Chinese food.

3. **A:** Do you wear your black slacks to school?

   B: No, I usually wear the gray one.

4. **A:** Do you wear the tie to work?

   B: No, I don't like the ties.

5. **A:** Do you have an white blazer?

   B: Yes, I do. Here's a small one and here's a large one.

6. **A:** Do you want a umbrella?

   B: No, I never use the umbrellas.

6 CONVERSATION COMPLETION

Complete the conversation. Use the words in the box. (Don't look at page 126 in your Student Book.)

a	look	one	size
an	~~May~~	ones	the
in	on	sale	up

CLERK: _____May_____ I help you?
1.

KEN: Yes, I'm looking for _____ new blazer.
2.

I have _____ interview tomorrow.
3.

CLERK: Oh, you're _____ luck! We're having a
4.

_____ on blazers.
5.

KEN: You are? Great!

CLERK: What _____?
6.

KEN: Forty-two.

CLERK: Okay. Be right back.

CLERK: All right. Do you like any of these?

KEN: Yes! I really like _____ blue one.
7.

CLERK: Do you want to try it _____?
8.

KEN: Sure.

CLERK: How does it feel?

KEN: Very comfortable. How does it _____,
9.

Laura?

LAURA: Well, it's pretty bright. And it's casual. How about

that black _____?
10.

It's more formal.

KEN: All the black _____ are dull—really boring.
11.

LAURA: Okay. It's _____ to you.
12.

CAN / CAN'T

1 AFFIRMATIVE AND NEGATIVE STATEMENTS WITH *CAN*

Complete the sentences. Use the words in the box.

bake	listen to the radio	run	sleep
cook	play golf	sit	swim

1. In a kitchen, we can _____bake_____, _____,

   _____, and _____.

   We can't ___play golf___, _____, _____, or

   _____.

2. At a beach, we can _____, _____, _____,

   _____, and _____.

   We can't _____, _____, or _____.

3. In a hospital, we can _____, _____, and

   _____.

   We can't _____, _____, _____,

   _____, or _____.

Complete this sentence. Use your own words.

4. In class, we can _____, _____, _____,

   and _____.

   We can't _____, _____, _____, or

   _____.

2 YES / NO QUESTIONS WITH CAN

Rewrite the requests. Use **can**.

1. Please do me a favor.

   Can you do me a favor, please?

2. Give Kathy this message, please.

   _____

3. Tell me the answers, please.

   _____

4. Call the police, please.

   _____

5. Please wait for me.

   _____

6. Help me with my homework, please.

   _____

3 AFFIRMATIVE AND NEGATIVE STATEMENTS WITH CAN

Complete the sentences on page 97. Use **can** *or* **can't** *and the words in parentheses.*

CAN THEY ...?	AMANDA	JUDY	STEVE	JOSH
SING	yes	no	no	yes
DANCE	yes	yes	no	no
SWIM	yes	yes	yes	no
DIVE	no	yes	no	no
WATER SKI	no	yes	no	no
SKI	no	no	yes	yes
PLAY THE GUITAR	yes	no	no	yes
PLAY THE PIANO	no	no	yes	yes

1. Amanda _____ *can sing* _____, and she _____ *can dance* _____.

   (sing / dance)

2. Josh _____ *can sing* _____, but he _____ *can't dance* _____.

   (sing / dance)

3. Steve and Josh _____, but they

   _____. (water ski / ski)

4. Judy _____, and she _____.

   (play the guitar / play the piano)

5. Judy _____, and she _____.

   (swim / dive)

6. Steve and Amanda _____, but they

   _____. (swim / dive)

7. Amanda _____, and she _____.

   (water ski / ski)

8. Amanda _____, but she _____.

   (play the guitar / play the piano)

9. I _____, _____ I _____.

   (sing / dance)

10. I _____, _____ I _____.

   (swim / dive)

④ YES / NO QUESTIONS WITH *CAN*

Write questions. Use **can**. *Then answer the questions. Use short answers.*

1. you / speak Mandarin

   ___ Can you speak Mandarin? ___   ___ Yes, I can. (OR: No, I can't.) ___

2. your teacher / speak Spanish

   _____   _____

(continued on next page)

3. your friends / play soccer

_____   _____

4. you / drive

_____   _____

5. your parents / speak English

_____   _____

6. your father / cook

_____   _____

7. you / sing well

_____   _____

8. your mother / play golf

_____   _____

5 **WH- QUESTIONS WITH *CAN***

Write questions. Use **can***. Then answer the questions.*

1. Where / I / get a good pizza

Where can I get a good pizza? _____

At Gino's Pizzeria. _____

2. How / I / learn your language

_____

_____

3. Who / change American dollars

_____

_____

4. Where / I / buy CDs

_____

_____

5. What / I / do on the weekend in your town

_____

_____

6 EDITING

Correct the conversation. There are eight mistakes. The first one is corrected for you.

A: I have a problem. ~~You can~~ _{Can you} help me?

B: Sure. How do can I help?

A: I can't not understand the homework. Can you understand it?

B: Yes, I do. But I can't to explain it well. Cans the teacher explain it to you?

A: I can't to find him.

B: He's in his office. I'm sure he can helps you.

UNIT

21 REVIEW: IMPERATIVE, PRESENT PROGRESSIVE, AND SIMPLE PRESENT

1 PRESENT PROGRESSIVE AND SIMPLE PRESENT: SHORT ANSWERS

Answer the questions. Write true short answers.

1. Are you sitting in a chair? _____Yes, I am._____

2. Do you know 100 words in English? _____Yes, I do._____

3. Do you often have homework? _____

4. Does your teacher have blonde hair? _____

5. Is your teacher helping you with this exercise? _____

6. Are your friends playing tennis at the moment? _____

7. Do you ever play tennis with your friends? _____

8. Does it often rain in your country? _____

9. Is it raining right now? _____

10. Are you having fun? _____

2 IMPERATIVES

Complete the suggestions for new students of English. Use the verbs in the box.

be	do	speak	write

1. _____Write_____ important new words in your notebook.

2. _____Don't write_____ every new word.

3. _____ your own language in class.

4. _____ English a lot in class.

5. _____ all your homework.

6. _____ afraid to ask questions.

3 PRESENT PROGRESSIVE VS. SIMPLE PRESENT

Complete the sentences. Use the correct tense of the verbs in parentheses.

1. This is George. He _____*lives*_____ near
                        (live)
    the beach. Right now he

    ___*is water skiing*___.
      (water ski)

2. This is Elena. She _____ the
                        (play)
    guitar. She _____ to play the
                        (love)
    guitar.

3. This is Joe. He _____ golf
                  (play)
    right now, but he _____ golf
                (not play)
    every day.

4. This is Mei Tan. She _____
                        (speak)
    three languages. Right now she and her
    friend _____ in Chinese.
        (talk)

(continued on next page)

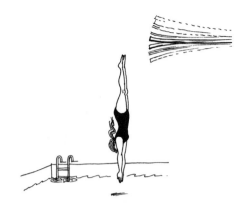

5. This is Sheila. She _____
(go)
swimming three or four times a week.

Right now she _____ into the
(dive)
pool.

6. This is Mr. Tomkins and his son. They

_____ chess. Mr. Tomkins
(play)

_____ more often than
(play)

his son.

---

4 **ACTION VS. NON-ACTION VERBS**

Complete the conversation. Use the words in parentheses and the correct tense.

A: ___Is anybody sitting___ here?
1. (anybody / sit)

B: _____ so.
2. (I / not think)

A: Who _____ to?
3. (this backpack / belong)

B: _____ Jack's.
4. (it / be)

A: Where _____?
5. (be / he)

B: _____ to the teacher.
6. (he / talk)

A: What _____ about?
7. (they / talk)

B: _____ a problem in the class.
8. (he / have)

A: _____. _____ happy in class.
9. (I / know)   10. (he / not look)

5 EDITING

Correct the conversations. There are ten mistakes. The first one is corrected for you.

1. **A:** What ~~are you doing~~ *do you do* every Monday?

   B: I'm go to English class.

2. **A:** Are you busy?

   B: Yes, I eat.

3. **A:** I'm hot.

   B: You open the window.

4. **A:** Are you wanting a cup of coffee right now?

   B: Yes, please. I'm needing a break.

5. **A:** Please don't you talk. You're being in a library.

   B: Sorry.

6. **A:** I'm liking your cousin. Introduce me to him.

   B: You can't talk to him in English. He isn't speaking English.

6 CONVERSATION COMPLETION

Complete the conversation. Use the words in the box. (Don't look at page 140 in your Student Book.)

are	Go	Is	She's
do	I'm	need	Show
Don't	Introduce	~~see~~	standing

TIM: Herb, do you ___*see*___ that woman over there?
1.

HERB: The blonde?

TIM: Uh-huh. _____ talking to Sabrina.
2.

HERB: _____ she wearing a gray suit?
3.

TIM: Yes, that's the woman. She's _____ next to the water fountain.
4.

_____ and talk to her. We need her business. _____ her our
5.   6.

new ads.

(continued on next page)

HERB: Me? _____ new here.
7.

TIM: Well, you _____ the practice.
8.

HERB: What do I say to her?

TIM: _____ yourself, ask about her new
9.

muffins, and show her our new ads.

HERB: Okay. She's walking this way . . . Wait a second. I

know her!

TIM: You _____?
10.

HERB: Yes. Her mom and my mom _____
11.

friends. That's Rita Jonas.

TIM: You're right. Beginner's luck! Give your mom a big

kiss. _____ forget.
12.

THE SIMPLE PAST: REGULAR VERBS (STATEMENTS)

---

1 AFFIRMATIVE AND NEGATIVE STATEMENTS WITH THE SIMPLE PAST

True or false? Write **T** *or* **F**.

____ **1.** I stayed home last night.

____ **2.** I didn't miss class two weeks ago.

____ **3.** The teacher arrived late to class last week.

____ **4.** I started my homework a few minutes ago.

____ **5.** I learned a lot in English class last week.

____ **6.** It didn't rain yesterday.

____ **7.** I didn't talk to my friends yesterday evening.

____ **8.** I didn't want to get out of bed yesterday morning.

2 AFFIRMATIVE STATEMENTS WITH THE SIMPLE PAST

Complete the sentences. Use the simple past of the verbs in the box. Put a check (✓) next to the things you did last night.

bake	listen	play	~~talk~~	visit	watch

_✓_ **1.** I ____talked____ on the phone for a long time.

____ **2.** I _____ TV all night.

____ **3.** I _____ to the radio.

____ **4.** I _____ cookies.

____ **5.** I _____ my grandparents.

____ **6.** I _____ computer games.

3 AFFIRMATIVE AND NEGATIVE STATEMENTS WITH THE SIMPLE PAST

Complete the sentences. Use the simple past.

1. I cook dinner at 6:00 every evening.

   I _____cooked_____ dinner at 6:00 yesterday evening.

2. I don't clean every day.

   I _____didn't clean_____ yesterday.

3. I arrive on time every day.

   I _____ on time yesterday.

4. Tim doesn't cook.

   He _____ last night.

5. Steve enjoys his class.

   He _____ his class last week.

6. Yuko and Omar study at the library every morning.

   They _____ at the library yesterday morning.

7. We call our children every weekend.

   We _____ our children last weekend.

8. The students ask a lot of questions in every class.

   They _____ a lot of questions in the last class.

9. We don't want to go to the movies tonight.

   We _____ to go to the movies last night.

10. I don't need anything from the store today.

    I _____ anything from the store yesterday.

4 PAST TIME EXPRESSIONS

Write the time expressions for the underlined words. (Look at page 260 in your Student Book for the months of the year.)

1. I liked the movie <u>on July 28</u>. _____ last week _____

2. I arrived in Seattle <u>on August 1</u>. _____ three days ago _____

3. We missed the party <u>on July 4</u>. _____

4. Maria graduated from college <u>on June 4</u>. _____

5. The children started school <u>on January 4</u>. _____

6. Judy stayed at a hotel <u>on August 3</u>. _____

7. Mark finished his report <u>on July 21</u>. _____

8. Herb talked to Rita <u>at night on August 3</u>. _____

9. My friend appeared on TV <u>in the morning on August 3</u>. _____

10. My cousin married John <u>on October 4</u>. _____

5 NEGATIVE STATEMENTS WITH THE SIMPLE PAST

Complete the sentences. Use the negative simple past of the verb.

1. I visited my parents, but I ____ didn't visit ____ my grandparents.

2. I watched TV, but I _____ a video.

(continued on next page)

3. She talked to her brother, but she _____ to her sister.

4. They enjoyed the movie, but they _____ the book.

5. We played cards, but we _____ chess.

6. He learned French, but he _____ Spanish.

6 AFFIRMATIVE AND NEGATIVE STATEMENTS WITH THE SIMPLE PAST

Complete the sentences. Use the simple past of the verbs in parentheses.

Yesterday was terrible. I _____missed_____ my train because my alarm clock
                          1. (miss)

_____. I _____ at the office late, and my boss _____ happy.
2. (not work)   **3. (arrive)**   **4. (not look)**

The big meeting _____ on time because of me, and it _____ late. The
                5. (not start)   **6. (finish)**

people at the meeting _____, but I know they _____ to finish early.
                      7. (not complain)   **8. (want)**

7 EDITING

Correct the e-mail message. There are six mistakes.

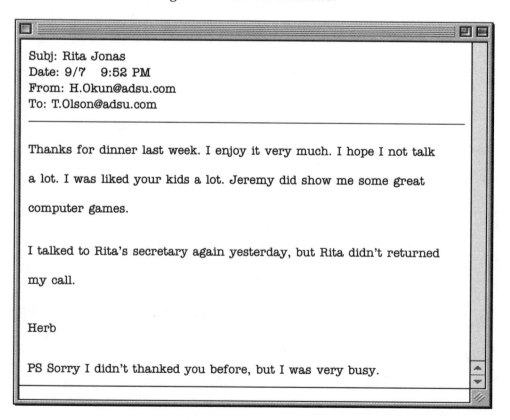

Subj: Rita Jonas
Date: 9/7   9:52 PM
From: H.Okun@adsu.com
To: T.Olson@adsu.com

Thanks for dinner last week. I enjoy it very much. I hope I not talk

a lot. I was liked your kids a lot. Jeremy did show me some great

computer games.

I talked to Rita's secretary again yesterday, but Rita didn't returned

my call.

Herb

PS Sorry I didn't thanked you before, but I was very busy.

THE SIMPLE PAST: REGULAR AND IRREGULAR VERBS

---

1 REGULAR VS. IRREGULAR VERBS WITH THE SIMPLE PAST

Complete the chart. Write the base form of the verb. Check (√) regular verb or *irregular verb.*

		BASE FORM OF VERB	REGULAR VERB	IRREGULAR VERB
1.	I <u>went</u> to a party last night.	go		√
2.	I <u>arrived</u> late.	arrive	√	
3.	Sam and Tanya <u>came</u> late too.			
4.	They <u>left</u> early.			
5.	I also <u>saw</u> Miranda at the party.			
6.	She <u>played</u> the guitar with Tom.			
7.	I <u>enjoyed</u> the music.			
8.	The food <u>was</u> great too.			
9.	I <u>ate</u> a lot.			
10.	I really <u>liked</u> the pizza.			
11.	I <u>talked</u> to a lot of old friends.			
12.	I <u>had</u> a lot of fun.			
13.	The party <u>ended</u> after midnight.			
14.	I <u>got</u> home at around 1:30 A.M.			

2 AFFIRMATIVE AND NEGATIVE STATEMENTS WITH IRREGULAR VERBS

Write sentences in the simple past.

1. (I / have breakfast / in the morning)   (I / not have / a big breakfast)

   I had breakfast in the morning _____ , but _____ I didn't have a big breakfast.

2. (I / drink / tea)   (I / not drink / coffee)

   _____ , but _____ .

3. (I / take / a bus / to class)   (I / not take / a train)

   _____ , but _____ .

4. (I / eat / lunch / in the school cafeteria)   (I / not eat / in a restaurant)

   _____ , but _____ .

5. (We / have / homework)   (we / not have / a lot of homework)

   _____ , but _____ .

6. (The teacher / put / the answers on the board) (he / not put / all the answers)

   _____ , but _____ .

7. (I / go / to the library after class)   (I / not go / with friends)

   _____ , but _____ .

8. (I / see / some classmates at the library)   (I / not see / the teacher)

   _____ , but _____ .

3 AFFIRMATIVE AND NEGATIVE STATEMENTS WITH IRREGULAR VERBS

Complete the sentences about yourself. Use the affirmative or negative simple past forms of the verbs in parentheses.

1. I _____ got up _____ early yesterday.
   (get up)

2. I _____ a test last week.
   (take)

3. I _____ well last night.
   (sleep)

4. My teacher _____ to my home last weekend.
    (come)

5. A friend _____ me a gift two days ago.
    (buy)

6. My family _____ on vacation last month.
    (go)

④ YES / NO QUESTIONS AND SHORT ANSWERS WITH THE SIMPLE PAST

Write yes / no questions about yesterday. Then answer the questions. Write true short answers.

1. I got up late today.

   Did you get up late yesterday?   Yes, I did. (OR: No, I didn't.)

2. The teacher drank coffee in class last week.

   _____   _____

3. My friends and I went to the movies last week.

   _____   _____

4. I ate breakfast today.

   _____   _____

5. I took a taxi today.

   _____   _____

6. My friends came to my home last week.

   _____   _____

7. I bought ice cream today.

   _____   _____

⑤ EDITING

Correct the conversations. There are eight mistakes. The first one is corrected for you.

            Did you sleep
1. A: ~~You did sleep~~ well last night?

   B: No, I wasn't.

2. A: I go on a picnic last Saturday.

   B: Did you have fun?

(continued on next page)

3. A: Did you eat anything at the party last night?

   B: No, and we not drink anything either.

4. A: I didn't saw my keys on the table.

   B: We putted them in your bag.

5. A: Did you went to school yesterday?

   B: Yes, I went.

---

6 CONVERSATION COMPLETION

Complete the conversation. Use the words in the box. (Don't look at page 152 in your Student Book.)

ate	didn't	snow	~~were~~
called	drank	Was	you
Did	happened	went	you're

KATHY: Hi, Amanda. Say, where ___*were*___ you and
1.
Josh on the weekend? I _____ several
2.
times.

AMANDA: Well, my dear, we had an adventure!

KATHY: You did?

AMANDA: Yes. We _____ out of town on Saturday.
3.
We left at 3:00. About 4:00 it started to

_____. In half an hour the snow was
4.
really deep.

KATHY: Oh no! Did _____ stop?
5.

AMANDA: Yeah. Then it got dark. We put on all our warm

clothes, so we were okay.

KATHY: _____ you have anything to eat?
6.

AMANDA: Yes, actually. We had some cookies and chocolate bars. We _____ those right away. And
7.
we had some sodas. We _____ them
8.
during the night.

KATHY: _____ it cold?
9.

AMANDA: Freezing! Fortunately, we had our sleeping bags. But we _____ sleep much.
10.

KATHY: Then what _____?
11.

AMANDA: In the morning a snowplow came along and cleared the road.

KATHY: Wow! Scary. I'm glad _____ okay.
12.

AMANDA: Thanks. Me too.

THE SIMPLE PAST:
WH- QUESTIONS

1 *WH-* QUESTIONS WITH THE SIMPLE PAST

Match the questions and answers.

_c_ **1.** What time did you get up?

____ **2.** Did you have breakfast?

____ **3.** Who made you breakfast?

____ **4.** Did you and your mother eat together?

____ **5.** What did you do after breakfast?

____ **6.** How did you get to the beach?

____ **7.** Where did you have lunch?

a. No, we didn't.

b. At the beach.

c. At 7:30.

d. I took the bus.

e. Yes, I did.

f. My mother.

g. I went to the beach.

2 AFFIRMATIVE AND NEGATIVE STATEMENTS WITH THE SIMPLE PAST

Complete the sentences. Use the simple past of the verbs in parentheses.

The accident at First and Main

_____happened_____ at 8:02. The driver of
　1. (happen)

a black BMW _____ at a
　　　　　　　　2. (stop)

green light because he _____
　　　　　　　　　　　3. (be)

lost. The driver of a white Toyota

_____ the BMW. The driver of the white Toyota
4. (hit)

_____ angry because the driver of the black BMW
5. (get)

_____ at a green light. They _____ a fight. Two
6. (stop)　　　　　　　　　　　　7. (have)

men on the street _____ up* the fight. A woman
　　　　　　　　8. (break)

_____ the driver of the black BMW to the hospital. He
9. (take)

_____ seriously hurt.
10. (not be)

*break up = stop

3 WH- QUESTIONS WITH THE SIMPLE PAST

Read the answers. Write questions about the accident in Exercise 2. Use **what**, **when**, **where**, **who**, *or* **why** *and the verbs in parentheses.*

1. (happen) __What happened at 8:02?__

   The accident at First and Main.

2. (happen) _____

   At 8:02.

3. (stop) _____

   The driver of a black BMW.

4. (stop) _____

   Because he was lost.

5. (hit) _____

   The driver of a white Toyota.

6. (get) _____

   Because the driver of the BMW stopped at a green light.

7. (get) _____ at?

   He got angry at the driver of the black BMW.

8. (have) _____

   A fight.

9. (have) _____

   The two drivers.

10. (break up) _____

    Two men on the street.

11. (take) _____

    To the hospital.

12. (take) _____

    A woman.

4 *WH-* QUESTIONS WITH THE SIMPLE PAST

Write questions. Then answer the questions.

1. what / you / study / in Unit 20

    What did you study in Unit 20?

    We studied "can" and "can't."

2. where / you / go / on the weekend

    _____

    _____

3. what / you / do / last night

    _____

    _____

4. who / you / talk to / yesterday

    _____

    _____

5. what / you / have / for homework last week

    _____

    _____

5 EDITING

Correct the conversations. There are eight mistakes. The first one is corrected for you.

1. **A:** What ~~had we~~ did we have for homework?

    B: Pages 90 and 91.

2. **A:** Who did build your house?

    B: My grandfather builded it.

3. **A:** Why did you got a letter from Steven Spielberg?

   B: Because I writed him and he answered my letter.

4. **A:** What happened at the game?

   B: The other team win.

5. **A:** What time the game began?

   B: It began late, at 2:30, because it rained.

6. **A:** How did the party be?

   B: Oh, we had a great time.

6 STATEMENTS AND QUESTIONS WITH THE SIMPLE PAST

Complete the conversation. Use the simple past of the words in parentheses.

AMANDA: ____I called____ you on the weekend, but _____ home. Where
     1. (I / call)   **2. (you / not be)**

_____?
3. (you / go)

KATHY: _____ to Mark's parents' house.
4. (we / go)

AMANDA: Oh? _____ there all weekend?
     5. (you / stay)

KATHY: Yes. _____ two nights there. _____ there on Friday night
     6. (we / spend)   **7. (we / fly)**

and _____ back last night.
8. (come)

AMANDA: What _____ there?
     9. (you / do)

KATHY: Well, on Saturday morning _____ home with Mark's parents
     10. (we / stay)

and _____.
11. (talk)

AMANDA: What _____ about?
     12. (you / talk)

(continued on next page)

KATHY: Lots of different things. _____ about funny things _____

13. (I / learn)   14. (Mark / do)

as a child and about other people in his family.

AMANDA: _____ anybody else in the family?

15. (you / meet)

KATHY: Yeah. In the evening, _____ a party for us.

16. (they / have)

AMANDA: Who _____?

17. (come)

KATHY: A lot of people—aunts, uncles, and cousins.

AMANDA: So _____ the whole family?

18. (you / meet)

KATHY: Just about.

AMANDA: _____ fun?

19. (it / be)

KATHY: Oh, yeah. _____ myself a lot.

20. (I / enjoy)

UNIT

25

SUBJECT AND OBJECT PRONOUNS

1 SUBJECT PRONOUNS

Rewrite the sentences. Use subject pronouns.

1. Carlos works in an office.

He works in an office.

2. Carlos and Tomiko need a ride.

3. My friends and I want to go to the party.

4. Kathy's car is small.

5. Bill invited a lot of people.

6. Carlos's wife didn't go to the party.

2 OBJECT PRONOUNS

Rewrite the sentences. Use object pronouns.

1. I didn't see Carlos.

I didn't see him.

2. I met Bill's wife.

(continued on next page)

3. I talked to Bill and Carlos.

_____

4. I didn't see Tomiko or Carlos's wife.

_____

5. They put the dog outside all night.

_____

6. Bill talked to me and my friend.

_____

3 OBJECT PRONOUNS

Complete the conversations. Use **me**, **you**, **him**, **her**, **it**, **us**, *or* **them**.

1. A: Here, Bill. This gift is for _____*you*_____.

   B: Thanks a lot.

2. A: Do you like Kathy's boyfriend?

   B: I don't know _____.

3. A: Kathy, would you like something to drink?

   B: Yes, please get _____ a soda.

4. A: How did Carlos and Tomiko get here?

   B: Kathy gave _____ a ride.

5. A: Carlos, can I use your cell phone?

   B: I don't have _____ here.

6. A: Bill, where is your wife?

   B: Carlos is talking to _____.

7. A: Tomiko, do you like these earrings?

   B: Yes, I like _____ very much.

8. A: You and your girlfriend didn't come to the party.

   B: That's because nobody invited _____.

④ SUBJECT AND OBJECT PRONOUNS

Write conversations. Put the words in the correct order.

1. **A:** _____ These chocolates are for you. _____   you / these / are / for / chocolates / .

   B: Thanks. _____ We love them. _____   them / we / love / .

2. **A:** _____   loves / she / you / .

   B: _____   her / don't / love / I / .

3. **A:** _____   the / give / keys / you / he / can / ?

   B: _____   he / them / find / can't / .

4. **A:** _____   you / I / can / help / ?

   B: _____   show / you / your / can /

   jackets / me / ?

5. **A:** _____   these / us / for / are / seats / ?

   B: _____   them / are / for / no / they / .

⑤ SUBJECT AND OBJECT PRONOUNS

Complete the conversations with subject and object pronouns.

1. **A:** Where are the chips?

   B: _____ They _____ are in the dining room. I put _____ them _____ on the table.

2. **A:** Did you invite Carlos and Tomiko? I like _____.

   B: Yes, _____ are coming with Kathy. _____ has a car.

3. **A:** Did you invite Mark?

   B: I invited _____, but _____ can't come.

4. **A:** This chair is heavy. I can't move _____. Can you help _____?

   B: Sure.

5. **A:** Oh, I hear the doorbell. Somebody's at the door. Can you open _____?

   B: _____ is already open.

(continued on next page)

6. A: Hello, Tomiko. It's nice to meet _____. Bill talks about _____ all

the time.

B: Really? Does _____ say nice things?

7. A: Bill, Tomiko is thirsty. Give _____ this soda.

B: But _____ is drinking some soda right now.

8. A: Bill, there are chocolates on the table. Are they for _____?

B: Yes, Carlos bought _____ for you and me.

6 EDITING

Correct the note. There are eight mistakes. The first one is corrected for you.

Dear Anne,

                     us
Thank you for inviting ~~we~~ to the party. The children and me had a great
time. The games were great. The kids loved they.

    Did Bob and Sally find the gifts? I left it in their room. Did Bob like the
tennis racquet? I bought it at Central Sports for he. I got Sally's soccer ball
there too. Does her still play soccer? (I know you said "No gifts." but what's a
birthday without gifts?)

    Why don't us meet one day for lunch? Give I a call.

Talk to you soon,

Sarah

7 CONVERSATION COMPLETION

Complete the conversation. Use the words in the box. (Don't look at page 166 in your Student Book.)

For	him	so	us
He	I	them	you
her	me	to	your

CARLOS: Well, Kathy, you're an American. What's a good gift?

KATHY: _____For_____ what?
1.

CARLOS: For the party at Bill's house on

Saturday. I want to get _____
2.

a gift.

KATHY: Right. Let me think.

CARLOS: How about flowers?

KATHY: Well, I suppose _____. But you don't usually give flowers
3.

_____ a man.
4.

CARLOS: He has a wife. Can I give them to _____?
5.

KATHY: Hmm. I'm not sure.

CARLOS: What about a CD of some cool Latin music? I know he likes music.

KATHY: No. Not appropriate. You don't give _____ boss a CD.
6.

CARLOS: Well, what do you suggest?

KATHY: Why don't you give _____ chocolates? _____ always eats
7.   8.

them at this desk.

CARLOS: Okay, good idea. A box of chocolates. Now, another question.

KATHY: What?

CARLOS: Tomiko and _____ need a ride to the party. Can you take
9.

_____?
10.

KATHY: For a price.

(continued on next page)

CARLOS: For a price? What do you mean?

KATHY: Get _____ a box of chocolates too.
11.

CARLOS: I don't believe you. You're not serious, are you?

KATHY: No, just kidding! See _____ at 6:30 on Saturday.
12.

HOW MUCH / HOW MANY

---

1 **HOW MUCH / HOW MANY**

Look at the picture of Steve's refrigerator. Write questions. Use **how many** *or* **how much** *and the words in parentheses. Then answer the questions. Use* **a lot**, **not many**, *or* **not much**.

1. (potatoes)

How many potatoes does Steve have? _____ A lot. _____

2. (oranges)

_____   _____

(continued on next page)

3. (bananas)

_____   _____

4. (milk)

_____   _____

5. (apples)

_____   _____

6. (fruit)

_____   _____

7. (soda)

_____   _____

8. (yogurt)

_____   _____

9. (juice)

_____   _____

10. (eggs)

_____   _____

2 HOW MUCH / HOW MANY

Answer the questions about your last vacation. Use numbers or the words in the box.

a lot	none	not many	not much

1. How many days were you away? _____

2. How much money did you spend? _____

3. How many postcards did you send? _____

4. How many people were with you? _____

5. How many suitcases did you take? _____

6. How much swimming did you do? _____

7. How many different restaurants did you eat at? _____

8. How much time were you alone? _____

3 GENERAL QUANTITY EXPRESSIONS

Complete the sentences. Use **a few**, **a little**, **many**, *or* **much**.

1. The hotel has _____*a few*_____ workers.

2. The hotel doesn't have _____*many*_____ parking spaces.

3. The hotel doesn't have _____ rooms.

4. It doesn't cost _____ money to stay at the hotel.

5. I have _____ information about the hotel.

6. The newspaper has _____ ads about the hotel.

7. The hotel rooms have _____ furniture in them.

8. You can watch _____ movies in your hotel room.

9. People don't eat _____ meals at the hotel.

10. People don't spend _____ time at the hotel.

4 EDITING

Correct the conversation. There are six mistakes. The first one is corrected for you.

A: How ~~many~~ *much* time do you get for vacation?

B: Four weeks.

A: Do you spend lot of time at home during your vacation?

B: No, only a little days.

A: Where do you usually go?

B: We spend a few time at my wife's parents' home. Then we go to the beach. We spend some time with our friends there.

A: How many friend do you see at the beach?

B: Not much. Four or five.

⑤ CONVERSATION COMPLETION

Complete the conversation. Use the words in the box. (Don't look at pages 172–173 in your Student Book.)

a	~~How~~	nothing	was
bet	many	people	way
did	much	time	were

JUDY: Welcome back.

AMANDA: Thanks.

MARK: _____How_____ was Ecuador?
             1.

JOSH: Great.

JUDY: How _____ days were you away?
                    2.

AMANDA: Ten. We _____ in Quito and the
                          3.
Galápagos Islands.

JUDY: The Galápagos Islands? Sounds exciting. How much _____ did you
                                                                   4.

spend there?

JOSH: Not _____. Only four days. But it _____ great. We took
              5.   **6.**

about _____ hundred photos. And we ate and slept on a boat.
         7.

MARK: Really? How many _____ were on the boat?
                              8.

AMANDA: Twelve including us. All very interesting people.

JUDY: I'll _____. How much _____ the trip cost?
              9.   **10.**

AMANDA: Almost _____. We won it on that Internet quiz show, "Who, What,
                      11.

Where, When, and Why."

JUDY: You're kidding!

AMANDA: No.

JUDY: Well, that's the _____ to go.
                            12.

THERE IS / THERE ARE, THERE WAS / THERE WERE

AFFIRMATIVE AND NEGATIVE STATEMENTS WITH *THERE IS / THERE ARE*

Look at the picture. Complete the sentences. Use **is**, **isn't**, **are**, *or* **aren't**.

1. There _____isn't_____ a woman at the table.

2. There _____is_____ a man at the table.

3. There _____ some fruit on the table.

4. There _____ any ice cream on the table.

5. There _____ any hamburgers on the table.

6. There _____ some milk on the table.

7. There _____ some eggs on the table.

8. There _____ a banana on the table.

9. There _____ an apple on the table.

10. There _____ any cheese on the table.

11. There _____ some muffins on the table.

12. There _____ any cookies on the table.

2 AFFIRMATIVE AND NEGATIVE STATEMENTS WITH *THERE IS / THERE ARE*

*Write sentences about your bedroom. Use **there** and the words in parentheses.*

1. (two beds) __There are two beds in my bedroom. (OR: There aren't two beds in my bedroom.)__

2. (rug) __There is a rug in my bedroom. (OR: There isn't a rug in my bedroom.)__

3. (television) _____

4. (computer) _____

5. (food) _____

6. (clothes) _____

7. (shoes) _____

8. (radio) _____

9. (books) _____

10. (money) _____

3 QUESTIONS AND ANSWERS WITH *THERE IS / THERE ARE*

*Look at the picture. Write questions. Use **there** and the words in parentheses. Then answer the questions.*

1. (men)

   __Are there any men in the picture?__   __Yes, there are.__

2. (women)

   _____   _____

3. (children)

_____   _____

4. (food)

_____   _____

5. (drinks)

_____   _____

6. (television)

_____   _____

7. (computer)

_____   _____

8. (furniture)

_____   _____

9. (car)

_____   _____

10. (books)

_____   _____

④ STATEMENTS AND QUESTIONS WITH _THERE WAS / THERE WERE_

Complete the conversation. Use **there was, there wasn't, there were, there weren't, was there,** _or_ **were there**.

A: Where were you on Saturday night?

B: ___There was___ a party at Steve's place.
         1.

A: How was it?

B: Really good. _____ great music, and _____ great food.
                    2.   **3.**

A: _____ pizza?
       4.

B: Of course, _____. You know Steve loves pizza.
                  5.

(continued on next page)

A: _____ a lot of people?
6.

B: Yes, _____.
7.

A: How many people _____?
8.

B: At least fifty. And Steve's apartment is very small. _____ any chairs, so we
9.

had to stand all night.

A: Didn't you dance?

B: No, _____ any space to dance. _____ one other problem.
10.   11.

A: What was that?

B: With all the music and people, _____ a lot of noise!
12.

⑤ EDITING

Correct the news report. There are six mistakes. The first one is corrected for you.

There ~~is~~ **was** a big fire last night.

There was at Eighth and Center

Streets. Years ago it was an

apartment building, but there

weren't any apartments there now.

That's why last night there was no

people in the building. Nobody

knows how the fire started. They

are many questions, but there

isn't any answers yet.

6 CONVERSATION COMPLETION

Complete the conversation. Use the words in the box. (Don't look at page 178 in your Student Book.)

are	~~go~~	there	wasn't
cars	it	They're	went
did	programs	was	were

BEN: Grandpa, did you _____ go _____ camping
1.
when you were a kid?

BILL: Sure we _____, Ben. We
2.
_____ camping a lot.
3.

ANNIE: How did you get there?

BILL: What do you mean, Annie?

ANNIE: Well, did you walk or ride a horse or what?

BILL: No, we drove to the camping areas.

ANNIE: Were there _____ back then,
4.
Grandpa?

BILL: Annie! Of course there were. I'm not *that* old!

BEN: What was _____ like when you were a kid, Grandma? Was there
5.
television?

MARY: Yes, _____ was, Ben. But TV _____ pretty new. There was
6. 7.
only one channel at first.

ANNIE: Only one channel? Really? How did you live?

MARY: It wasn't hard. There were a lot of good _____ on that channel.
8.

ANNIE: Grandpa, are things better now than when you were a kid?

BILL: Well, there _____ much stress. People didn't worry so much.
9.

MARY: And there _____ fun things to do.
10.

BILL: Like free concerts and baseball games.

BEN: Grandma, _____ there any more hot dogs?
11.

MARY: Yes, there are. _____ in the cooler.
12.

UNIT 28 DESCRIPTIVE ADJECTIVES

1 VOCABULARY

Complete the crossword puzzle.

ACROSS

5. enjoying a good time
10. good at one sport or a lot of sports
11. not full of fun
12. liking things that younger people like
13. showing great feelings of love
14. good at learning, understanding, and thinking about things

DOWN

1. not wanting to spend money
2. not friendly
3. good at drawing, for example
4. good, helpful; wanting to do things that make other people happy
6. not telling the truth
7. not easily worried
8. giving what you can, for example, money or time
9. not kind or helpful

2 SENTENCES WITH ADJECTIVE + NOUN

Unscramble the word groups to write sentences.

1. a / she / man / for / looking / rich / is / .

   She is looking for a rich man.

2. like / serious / women / you / do / why / ?

3. an / I / man / want / athletic / .

4. very / man / generous / that / is / .

5. talking / woman / they / interesting / an / are / to / .

6. couple / they / happy / are / a / .

7. you / good-looking / any / know / men / do / ?

8. funny / honest / his / wasn't / or / personal ad / .

3 DESCRIPTIVE ADJECTIVES

Combine the sentences.

1. He is an older man. He is fun-loving.

   He is a fun-loving older man.

2. Venus and Serena Williams are tennis players. They are famous.

3. Jessica and Tim live in a house. The house is big.

4. Josh and Amanda ate at a restaurant. The restaurant was awful.

(continued on next page)

5. Judy likes movies. The movies are sad.

_____

6. Buy this CD player. The CD player is cool.

_____

7. Jeremy bought a CD player. The CD player was expensive.

_____

8. Bill and Mark have jobs. The jobs are important.

_____

4 DESCRIPTIVE ADJECTIVES WITH PLURAL NOUNS

Rewrite the sentences. Make the nouns plural. Make all the other necessary changes.

1. The personal ad is funny. _The personal ads are funny._____

2. He is an interesting man. _____

3. The black dog is friendly. _____

4. The expensive car is over there. _____

5. The artistic student is a young Italian. _____

6. The boring book has a red cover. _____

7. The good-looking actor is from China. _____

5 DESCRIPTIVE ADJECTIVES

*Write sentences. Use words from columns **A**, **D**, and **E** only one time.*

A	B	C	D	E
Matt Damon			big	actor
Beijing and Mexico City			British	artist
Ferraris and BMWs			expensive	cars
Prince Harry and Prince William	is	(a)	American	city
Quebec	are		Japanese	cities
Sushi	was	(an)	old	book
The Beatles	were		poor	food
The Bible			small	men
Van Gogh			young	singers

1. <u>Matt Damon is an American actor.</u>

2. _____

3. _____

4. _____

5. _____

6. _____

7. _____

8. _____

9. _____

6 EDITING

Correct the conversation. There are seven mistakes. The first one is corrected for you.

A: Where were you last night?

B: I had a date.

A: Really?

B: Yeah. I met $\overset{a}{\wedge}$beautiful woman through a personal ad.

A: Oh, yeah? Tell me about her. Is she an athletic like you?

B: Yeah. She plays three differents sports.

A: What else?

B: Well, she's a person very funny, and she listens to olds songs like me.

A: Does she work?

B: Yeah. She has a interesting job with a music company.

A: She sounds like she's the woman perfect for you.

B: She is.

COMPARATIVE ADJECTIVES

1 REGULAR AND IRREGULAR COMPARATIVE ADJECTIVES

Write the adjectives.

1. bigger _____big_____

2. cheaper _____

3. dirtier _____

4. easier _____

5. hotter _____

6. larger _____

7. quicker _____

8. taller _____

9. better _____

10. worse _____

2 SHORT AND LONG ADJECTIVES

Write the words in the correct columns.

~~active~~	artistic	boring	busy	cold	dark
difficult	exciting	expensive	friendly	funny	healthy
honest	important	interesting	old	short	warm

ONE SYLLABLE	TWO SYLLABLES ENDING IN –y	TWO SYLLABLES NOT ENDING IN –y	MORE THAN TWO SYLLABLES
		active	

❸ COMPARATIVE ADJECTIVES

Complete the sentences. Use the comparative form of the adjectives.

1. This book is interesting, but the other book is ___more interesting___.

2. I'm busy on Mondays, but I'm _____ on Tuesdays.

3. Unit 28 was difficult, but Unit 29 is _____.

4. Julia is short, but her sister is _____.

5. The movie is funny, but the book is _____.

6. The cake is good, but the ice cream is _____.

7. This book is boring, but that book is _____.

8. My grandfather is active, but my grandmother is _____.

9. The traffic today is bad, but the traffic yesterday was _____.

10. It's cold today, but it was _____ yesterday.

❹ COMPARATIVE ADJECTIVES + *THAN*

Make comparisons. Use the words in parentheses.

1. China is ___bigger than___ Japan. (big / small)

2. Thailand is _____ Korea. (cold / hot)

3. Chinese is _____ English. (easy / hard)

4. London is _____ New York. (old / young)

5. The weather in Australia is _____ the weather in Canada. (bad / good)

6. Tokyo is _____ Quebec. (crowded / empty)

7. The Nile River is _____ the Amazon River. (long / short)

8. The traffic in big cities is _____ the traffic in small cities. (bad / good)

➎ QUESTIONS WITH *WHICH*

Write questions. Use **which***. Then answer the questions.*

1. expensive / computers or cell phones

    Which are more expensive, computers or cell phones?   Computers.

2. easy / swimming or water skiing

_____   _____

3. fast / planes or trains

_____   _____

4. warm / January or July

_____   _____

5. popular / around the world / soccer or baseball

_____   _____

6. good / for you / cake or fruit

_____   _____

➏ EDITING

Correct the conversation. There are eight mistakes. The first one is corrected for you.

A: So how's your new apartment? Is it ~~more good~~ ^{better} than your old one?

B: Yes, it is. It's biger and more cheap.

A: And where is it? Is the location good?

B: Oh, yeah. It's near the train station, so it's more easy to get to work. And I like the
neighborhood too. It has a lot of trees and is beautifuler. The neighborhood is also
more cleaner.

A: How many bedrooms are there?

B: Well, there are three bedrooms. One bedroom is smaller from the other two. It's noisyer
too. But the rest of the apartment is perfect. Why don't you come and see it this
weekend?

A: That sounds like a good idea.

7 CONVERSATION COMPLETION

Complete the conversation. Use the words in the box. (Don't look at page 192 in your Student Book.)

~~about~~	entertainment	more	real
better	food	of	than
cheaper	got	older	worse

KEN: So when's the party?

LAURA: Saturday night. It starts ____about____ eight.
                    1.

MARTY: How many people are coming?

LAURA: I've _____ fifteen on the list.
        2.

MARTY: What about music? I can bring my rap and

metal CDs.

KEN: Get _____! We want to dance, right? Rap
        3.

is bad for dancing, and metal is _____.
                           4.

CELINE: Let's have rock. It's a lot _____ for
                     5.

dancing.

LAURA: Okay. My _____ brother has a lot of rock
                6.

CDs. Now, what about _____?
                   7.

KEN: How about steak? We can barbecue some steak.

CELINE: Pizza's easier and quicker _____ steak.
                     8.

And it's _____.
         9.

KEN: Okay, sounds good. And what about

_____? Besides dancing, I mean.
   10.

MARTY: How about watching some videos?

LAURA: Well . . . I'm tired _____ them. Games are
               11.

_____ interesting than videos.
   12.

SUPERLATIVE ADJECTIVES

	1	REGULAR AND IRREGULAR COMPARATIVE AND SUPERLATIVE ADJECTIVES

Complete the chart.

	ADJECTIVE	COMPARATIVE ADJECTIVE	SUPERLATIVE ADJECTIVE
1.	athletic	more athletic	the most athletic
2.	bad		
3.	big		
4.	boring		
5.	busy		
6.	clean		
7.	difficult		
8.	easy		
9.	good		
10.	healthy		
11.	honest		
12.	hot		
13.	intelligent		
14.	popular		

2 SUPERLATIVE ADJECTIVES

Compare the three things, places, or people in the pictures. Use the words in parentheses.

| **The Mercedes E500** | **The BMW Mini** | **The Lincoln Navigator** |

1. (small / car) _The BMW Mini is the smallest car._

2. (expensive / car) _____

3. (large / car) _____

| **Quebec** | **Istanbul** | **New York** |

4. (cold / city) _____

5. (large / city) _____

6. (old / city) _____

| **Cheetahs** | **Elephants** | **Lions** |

7. (fast / animal) _____

8. (dangerous / animal) _____

9. (heavy / animal) _____

(continued on next page)

Andy Warhol

Princess Diana

Mother Teresa

10. (artistic / person) _____

11. (pretty / person) _____

12. (poor / person) _____

---

❸ SUPERLATIVE ADJECTIVES

Write questions. Use the superlative form of the adjectives. Then answer the questions.

1. What / be / long / river / in the world

　　<u>What's the longest river in the world?</u>　　　　<u>The Nile River.</u>

2. What / be / expensive / restaurant / in your town

　　_____　　_____

3. What / be / bad / month / for a vacation

　　_____　　_____

4. Who / be / tall / person / in your class

　　_____　　_____

5. Who / be / young / person / in your class

　　_____　　_____

6. Who / be / popular / singer / in your country

　　_____　　_____

7. What / be / funny / program / on TV

　　_____　　_____

8. What / be / cold / month / of the year

_____   _____

9. Who / be / beautiful / actress / in your country

_____   _____

❹ EDITING

Correct the paragraphs. There are eight mistakes. The first one is corrected for you.

> I like my class. I have the ~~most good~~ ^{best} teacher in the
> school, but our class is in the baddest room. Last
> year I was in the largest room. Now I'm in
> smallest.
>
> There are ten students in the class. The most nicest
> is Ram. He's really friendly. The most funny is Elisa.
> The intelligentest is Songkit, and the most
> artistic is Carlos.
>
> We do lots of different things in class. The
> more interesting activities are the group
> discussions. The boringest part of the class is
> the homework. I really don't like homework.

❺ CONVERSATION COMPLETION

Complete the conversation. Use the words in the box. (Don't look at page 198 in your Student Book.)

best	most	quickest	strangest
~~dream~~	of	scooter	the
in	on	strange	way

(continued on next page)

JUDY: I had a really strange _____dream_____
1.
last night.

MARK: You always have _____ dreams.
2.

JUDY: Yes, but this one was the _____
3.
dream of all.

MARK: Tell me about it.

THE COLDEST DAY OF THE YEAR

JUDY: Okay. I was in New York City on a very cold day. The paper said it was the coldest

day _____ the year. I was late for a concert. I asked a guy, "What's
4.

_____ quickest way to get to 33rd Street and Seventh Avenue?" He said,
5.

"The _____ way isn't the best way. The _____ way is with me."
6.   7.

MARK: So did you go with him?

JUDY: Uh-huh. We rode together on his

_____. At times the
8.
scooter went up in the air. It was the

_____ wonderful
9.
ride _____ the world.
10.
We laughed the whole way there.

MARK: And then?

JUDY: Well, then I woke up. But that's not all.

MARK: Listen, it's getting late. Tell me the rest on the _____ to class.
11.

JUDY: Oops! You're right. Come _____. Let's go.
12.

PREPOSITIONS OF TIME:
IN, ON, AT

 1 PREPOSITIONS OF TIME

Write the words in the correct columns.

the afternoon	lunchtime	October 4, 2002
April	May	a quarter after two
the evening	the morning	Thursday
four o'clock	night	Tuesday
half past eleven	1990	weekdays
June 1st	November 3rd	the weekend

AT	IN	ON
lunchtime	the afternoon	October 4, 2002

❷ DATES

Write the dates in words.

1.

Oct.						
S	M	T	W	T	F	S
			1	2	3	4
5	6	7	8	9	10	11
12	13	14	15	16	17	18
19	20	21	(22)	23	24	25
26	27	28	29	30	31	

2.

Feb.						
S	M	T	W	T	F	S
						1
(2)	3	4	5	6	7	8
9	10	11	12	13	14	15
16	17	18	19	20	21	22
23	24	25	26	27	28	

3.

Apr.						
S	M	T	W	T	F	S
		1	2	3	4	5
6	7	8	9	10	11	12
13	14	15	16	17	18	19
20	21	22	23	24	25	26
27	28	29	(30)			

4.

Dec.						
S	M	T	W	T	F	S
	1	2	3	4	5	6
7	8	9	10	11	12	13
14	15	16	17	18	19	20
21	22	23	24	25	26	27
28	29	30	(31)			

5.

Sept.						
S	M	T	W	T	F	S
	(1)	2	3	4	5	6
7	8	9	10	11	12	13
14	15	16	17	18	19	20
21	22	23	24	25	26	27
28	29	30				

6.

Jan.						
S	M	T	W	T	F	S
			1	2	(3)	4
5	6	7	8	9	10	11
12	13	14	15	16	17	18
19	20	21	22	23	24	25
26	27	28	29	30	31	

7.

Aug.						
S	M	T	W	T	F	S
					1	2
3	4	5	6	7	8	(9)
10	11	12	13	14	15	16
17	18	19	20	21	22	23
24	25	26	27	28	29	30
31						

8.

Nov.						
S	M	T	W	T	F	S
						1
2	3	4	5	6	7	8
9	10	(11)	12	13	14	15
16	17	18	19	20	21	22
23	24	25	26	27	28	29
30						

9.

Mar.						
S	M	T	W	T	F	S
						1
2	3	4	5	6	7	8
9	10	11	12	13	14	15
16	17	18	19	20	21	22
23	24	(25)	26	27	28	29
30	31					

1. It's October twenty-second.

2. _____

3. _____

4. _____

5. _____

6. _____

7. _____

8. _____

9. _____

❸ PREPOSITIONS OF TIME

Complete the conversation. Use **at,** **in,** *or* **on.**

LIZA: I'd like information about flights to Vancouver.

AGENT: When would you like to go?

LIZA: I'm not sure. I'd like to go _____in_____ September—either _____
1.   2.

September 19th or _____ September 20th.
3.

AGENT: Well, September 19th is _____ Sunday, so the ticket is cheaper. Tickets
4.

_____ weekdays are more expensive than tickets _____ the
5.   6.

weekends.

LIZA: Really? Well, when are there flights _____ Sunday, September 19th?
7.

AGENT: There's one _____ 7:00 _____ the morning, another
8.   9.

_____ noon, one flight _____ the afternoon _____
10.   11.   12.

3:30, and another one _____ nine _____ night.
13.   14.

❹ TIME EXPRESSIONS

Answer the questions. Write true long answers. Use **at,** **in,** *or* **on.**

1. What time do you get up? __I get up at 7:30 in the morning._____

2. What time do you usually go to bed? _____

3. What year were you born? _____

4. What month were you born? _____

5. When is your birthday? _____

6. When did your parents get married? _____

7. What time does English class start and end? _____

8. What days do you have English class? _____

5 EDITING

Correct the conversations. There are eight mistakes. The first one is corrected for you.

1. A: When does class start?

       At
B: ~~On~~ 2:00.

2. A: Is your birthday on May?

  B: Yes, it is. It's on May 20th.

3. A: Do you ever work at the night?

  B: Sometimes. But I usually work in morning and afternoon.

4. A: When is your flight?

  B: It's in five o'clock at the morning.

5. A: What do you do in weekends?

  B: In Sundays I go to my grandparents' home for dinner.

6 CONVERSATION COMPLETION

Complete the conversation. Use the words in the box. (Don't look at page 204 in your Student Book.)

afternoon	~~calling~~	in	Saturday
at	doing	looking	two-story
back	fun	on	yourselves

TIM: Tim Olson.

FELIX: Hello, Tim! This is Felix Maxa ____calling____. Do

                                      1.

  you remember me? We met _____ August

                                        2.

  on the train to Seattle.

TIM: Felix! Of course! It's great to hear from you. How are

  you _____?

             3.

FELIX: Wonderful. Say, I called to invite you and your wife

  to our house for a barbecue.

TIM: Hey, that sounds like _____. We'd really like that. When is it?

                            4.

FELIX: On _____, the 20th. In the _____.
                    5.   **6.**

TIM: I think we're free. But I need to check with Jessica. Can I call you _____?
                                                                                          7.

FELIX: Sure.

[Later]

FELIX: Hello?

TIM: Hi, Felix. This is Tim. We're free _____ the 20th. We can come to the
                                                              8.

barbecue.

FELIX: Great!

TIM: What's the address?

FELIX: We're at 819 Fortieth Avenue. From Forty-fifth, turn left on Stone Way and then

right on Fortieth. It's the third house on the right, a light blue _____.
                                                                                         9.

TIM: Okay. What time?

FELIX: About 2:30.

TIM: Great. Can we bring anything?

FELIX: Just _____.
                       10.

TIM: Okay, thanks a lot. I'm _____ forward to it. See you on Saturday
                                                11.

_____ 2:30. 'Bye.
        12.

32 THE FUTURE WITH *BE GOING TO*: STATEMENTS

1 PRESENT PROGRESSIVE VS. THE FUTURE WITH *BE GOING TO*

Which sentences describe the pictures? Circle the correct answers.

1. **(a.)** He's sleeping.

    b. He's going to sleep.

2. **a.** It's raining.

    b. It's going to rain.

3. **a.** He's falling.

    b. He's going to fall.

4. **a.** She's putting the book down.

    b. She's going to put the book down.

5. **a.** He's watching TV.

    b. He's going to watch TV.

6. **a.** She's buying something.

    b. She's going to buy something.

2 AFFIRMATIVE STATEMENTS WITH *BE GOING TO*

What are the people going to do? Write sentences about the future. Use the words in the box.

buy some food	exercise	have lunch	teach
see a movie	sleep	~~swim~~	

1. Judy and Bob are going to the beach.

　　They're going to swim.

2. Amanda and Josh are going to a movie theater.

3. Annie's going to her bedroom.

4. Tim's going into a restaurant.

5. Mary and Bill are going into a supermarket.

6. Steve's going into his classroom.

7. Kathy's going to a gym.

3 NEGATIVE STATEMENTS WITH *BE GOING TO*

Write negative sentences about this week.

1. The Olsons bought a house last week.

　　They're not going to buy a house this week.

2. I spent a lot of money last week.

3. My friends and I were absent from class last week.

(continued on next page)

4. Steve went on a class trip with his students last week.

_____

5. Mark and Kathy got married last week.

_____

6. Jeremy took a test last week.

_____

7. Laura had a party last week.

_____

④ AFFIRMATIVE AND NEGATIVE STATEMENTS WITH *BE GOING TO*

Write sentences about your activities next weekend. Use the words in parentheses.

1. (clean my home) ____I'm going to clean my home next weekend. (OR: I'm not going to

clean my home next weekend.)____

2. (eat out) _____

3. (go out with friends) _____

4. (go shopping) _____

5. (go to the movies) _____

6. (play soccer) _____

7. (study) _____

8. (visit relatives) _____

9. (wake up early) _____

10. (work) _____

5 EDITING

Correct the paragraph. There are six mistakes. The first one is corrected for you.

I can't believe the course is almost over.
It's going to finish in one week. Most of my
classmates are going return home, but some
are no going to leave. Rana going to start a
new job. Misha is going to taking another course.
Masao and Laura is going to get married, and
I'm going to go to their wedding.

6 CONVERSATION COMPLETION

Complete the conversation. Use the words in the box. (Don't look at page 212 in your Student Book.)

~~be~~	doing	have	not
chill	faster	hurry	start
come	going	jam	to

LAURA: Ken, hurry up! We're going to _____be_____ late!
1.

KEN: What's the _____? It's just a silly little soccer
2.

game!

LAURA: It's not silly, and it's not little. Sam's on the team! It's a

big game. I think they're _____ to win.
3.

KEN: I know. That's what you told me. Is your brother a

pretty good player?

LAURA: He's really good.

KEN: Do I need an umbrella?

LAURA: No. It's _____ going to rain . . . Come on.
4.

[Later]

(continued on next page)

LAURA: Can't you drive any _____?
5.

KEN: I'm already _____ the speed limit. But how
6.

_____ you like soccer so much?
7.

LAURA: It's a great game. A lot of people can play it. You don't

_____ to be a giant.
8.

KEN: But is it a real sport? Take basketball or baseball.

Those are sports.

LAURA: Soccer is the most popular sport in the world.

KEN: Well, it's not the most popular sport in *my* world.

LAURA: Oh, no! A traffic _____! The game's going to _____ soon.
9.   10.

KEN: Laura, _____ out! We're going _____ make it on time.
11.   12.

THE FUTURE WITH *BE GOING TO*: *YES / NO* QUESTIONS

1 YES/NO QUESTIONS WITH THE FUTURE WITH *BE GOING TO*

Complete the conversations. Use the questions in the box.

Are they going to get married?	~~Are you going to go to~~ bed?
Are they going to take a trip?	Is he going to buy a new one?
Are they going to win?	Is he going to study?
Are you going to buy her a gift?	Is his father going to drive him?
Are you going to eat out?	

1. A: I'm tired.

    B: _Are you going to go to bed?_

2. A: Jeremy's late for school.

    B: _____

3. A: We don't have any food in the house.

    B: _____

4. A: Ben has a test tomorrow.

    B: _____

5. A: It's Annie's birthday on Saturday.

    B: _____

6. A: Kathy and Mark are in love.

    B: _____

7. A: Judy's team is playing well.

    B: _____

(continued on next page)

8. A: Steve's computer is old.

B: _____

9. A: Tim and Jessica are putting clothes in suitcases.

B: _____

❷ FUTURE TIME EXPRESSIONS

Imagine that it is Sunday, May 1, 2015. Write the time expressions for the underlined words. Use the words in the box.

~~next week~~	next month	next year
in five days	in three months	in two years

1. We're going to finish school <u>on May 8th</u>. _____ next week _____

2. They're going to get married <u>in 2017</u>. _____

3. We're going to take our vacation <u>in August</u>. _____

4. She's going to move <u>on June 8th</u>. _____

5. I'm going to visit you <u>on May 6th</u>. _____

6. He's going to graduate <u>in 2016</u>. _____

❸ YES / NO QUESTIONS AND SHORT ANSWERS WITH *BE GOING TO*

Write yes / no *questions. Use* **be going to***. Then answer the questions. Use short answers.*

1. it / rain / tonight

_____ Is it going to rain tonight? _____   _____ Yes, it is. (OR: No, it isn't.) _____

2. you / do something with friends / next weekend

_____   _____

3. your teacher / give homework / next week

_____   _____

4. you and your classmates / study together / tomorrow

_____   _____

5. you / watch TV / tonight

_____   _____

6. the post office / be open / tomorrow

_____   _____

7. your friends / play cards with you / next Saturday

_____   _____

8. you and your family / spend time together / next weekend

_____   _____

9. the weather / be good / tomorrow

_____   _____

10. you / take a trip / next month

_____   _____

11. your parents / move / next year

_____   _____

12. you / be busy / next week

_____   _____

4 EDITING

Correct the conversation. There are nine mistakes. The first one is corrected for you.

MARY: Hi, Annie. It's Grandma. How are you?

ANNIE: Okay. Grandma, are you going to visit us this weekend?

MARY: No, I'm not going. I going to visit Uncle Steve.

ANNIE: Grandpa going to go with you?

MARY: Yes, he's. Why?

(continued on next page)

ANNIE: Because I'm bored. Mom has a new job, and we never do anything fun.

MARY: Let me talk to your mother.

ANNIE: She isn't here. She going being late tonight. Do you want to talk to Jeremy?

MARY: Why? Where's your dad? He is going to be late tonight too?

ANNIE: Yeah. They're both going to come home late.

MARY: Well, don't worry. I'm talking to both of them.

5 CONVERSATION COMPLETION

Complete the conversation. Use the words in the box. (Don't look at page 218 in your Student Book.)

Actually	be	How	isn't
am	day	I'm	It's
Are	going	Is	same

JESSICA: _____How_____ was work, Tim?
              1.

  TIM: Same old, _____ old. How was
                      2.

          your _____?
                  3.

JESSICA: _____, I had an interesting call.
              4.

  TIM: Oh?

JESSICA: You know Dan Evans, the TV producer? Well,

          he has an idea for a new show.

  TIM: What kind?

JESSICA: Another news program.

  TIM: Really?

JESSICA: Uh-huh. _____ going to be on national TV, and he wants me to be in it.
                      5.

JEREMY: Awesome! _____ you going to have a big part?
                      6.

JESSICA: Yes, I _____. I'm going to _____ the main reporter.
                    7.   8.

JEREMY: That's so cool.

  TIM: Hmm . . . _____ it going to mean a lot of travel?
                      9.

JESSICA: I think so.

ANNIE: Don't take it, Mom. I don't want you to travel.

BEN: Yeah. Who's _____ to help me with my homework?
10.

TIM: Hey, guys. _____ still going to be here.
11.

JESSICA: Anyway, kids, don't worry . . . The show _____ going to air for
12.

a long time.

THE FUTURE WITH *BE GOING TO*: *WH-* QUESTIONS

① *WH-* QUESTIONS WITH *BE GOING TO*

Answer the questions. Write true sentences.

1. What time are you going to go to bed tonight?

   _____

2. Where are you going to go tomorrow morning?

   _____

3. Who are you going to see tomorrow?

   _____

4. What are you going to do next weekend?

   _____

5. How is your next class going to be?

   _____

6. Who is going to be absent in your next class?

   _____

7. When is your next test going to be?

   _____

   _____

② QUESTION WORDS

Read the answers. Write the correct question words. Use **how, what, when, where, who,** *or* **why.**

1. ___What___?   They're going to play tennis.
2. _____?   Angry.
3. _____?   In ten minutes.
4. _____?   The couple in the car.
5. _____?   Into the movie theater.

6. _____?   The man in the black shirt.
7. _____?   Because he's going to buy a pair of shoes.
8. _____?   The woman's wallet.

3 WH- QUESTIONS WITH *BE GOING TO*

Write questions. Use **be going to**. *Then find an answer for each question in Exercise 2.*

1. Who / get / a ticket

   __Who is going to get a ticket?__   __The couple in the car.__

2. What / the two people in the car / do

   _____   _____

3. Who / take / the woman's wallet

   _____   _____

4. What / the man in the black shirt / take

   _____   _____

(continued on next page)

5. How / the woman / feel

_____   _____

6. Why / the man in the hat / go / into the store

_____   _____

7. Where / the people in line / go

_____   _____

8. When / the movie / start

_____   _____

4 WH- QUESTIONS WITH *BE GOING TO*

Complete the conversations. Write questions. Use **how, what, when, where,** *or* **who** *and the words in parentheses.*

1. A: Kathy and Mark got engaged last week.

   B: (get married) _When are they going to get married?_____

   A: Next June, I think.

2. A: Kathy's parents are going to have an engagement party for her and Mark.

   B: (invite) _____

   A: Lots of relatives and friends.

3. A: I'm going to go to the supermarket.

   B: (buy) _____

   A: Some soda, some ice cream, and some other things for the party.

4. A: We're going to go to the beach next Saturday.

   B: (get there) _____

   A: One of my friends has a car.

5. A: Judy's going to take a trip during her vacation.

   B: (go) _____

   A: Two or three places in Mexico.

6. A: The car's dirty.

   B: (clean it) _____

   A: You are!

⑤ EDITING

Correct the conversation. There are six mistakes. The first one is corrected for you.

A: Did you hear the news? Amanda's pregnant.

B: Really? When ~~she is~~ *is she* going to have the baby?

A: At the end of January. She's going to stop working in the middle of December.

B: Why is she stop working?

A: Because she going to be very busy with the baby.

B: How are going to have enough money she and Josh?

A: Josh has a good job.

B: What is she and Josh going to name the baby?

A: I have no idea.

B: Where they going to live? Their apartment is so small.

A: I think they're going to move.

6   CONVERSATION COMPLETION

Complete the conversation. Use the words in the box. (Don't look at page 224 in your Student Book.)

are	have	say	~~what's~~
Congratulations	How	took	yeah
engaged	marry	What	You're

KATHY: Mark, _____what's_____ bothering you? You look pretty
1.

nervous.

MARK: I *am* nervous. _____ am I going to say this?
2.

KATHY: Say what?

MARK: Well, I have something important to _____.
3.

KATHY: Let me guess . . . _____ going to move away.
4.

Or . . . maybe you're going to visit your grandmother in

Nashville.

MARK: No. This is about us . . . Will you _____ me?
5.

KATHY: Well . . . I only have one thing to say.

MARK: Oh, no. What?

KATHY: What _____ you so long to ask?
6.

[Later]

MARK: Hello?

JOSH: Hey, Mark. This is Josh. _____ are you going
7.

to do on Sunday?

MARK: No plans. Why?

JOSH: A bunch of us _____ going to watch the big
8.

game. Do you want to come?

MARK: Well, yeah, I think so. By the way, Kathy and I _____ some big news.
9.

JOSH: Oh _____? What?
10.

MARK: We're _____.
11.

JOSH: What? That's great, man! _____!
12.

MARK: Thanks. Tell you about it on Sunday. So what time is the party going to start?

UNIT

35

SUGGESTIONS: *LET'S*...,
WHY DON'T WE...?

1 SUGGESTIONS WITH *LET'S*... AND *WHY DON'T WE*...?

Where are the people? Match the suggestions and places.

___e___ **1.** Why don't we park over there?

_____ **2.** Let's put the TV near the window.

_____ **3.** Why don't we order some steak?

_____ **4.** Let's not sit near the water.

_____ **5.** Let's finish the report tomorrow.

_____ **6.** Why don't we buy Bob this game?

_____ **7.** Let's put our tent under this tree.

_____ **8.** Let's not leave the camera in the room.

a. The people are at the beach.

b. The people are at work.

c. The people are in a store.

d. The people are in a hotel.

e. The people are in a car.

f. The people are in their new home.

g. The people are in a restaurant.

h. The people are at a campsite.

2 SUGGESTIONS WITH *LET'S*...

Complete the conversations. Circle the correct sentences and write them on the lines.

1. A: It's Jessica and Tim's anniversary next week.

   B: ___Let's send them a card.___

   (**a.**) Let's send them a card.   **b.** Let's not send them a card.

2. A: The weather's terrible.

   B: _____

   a. Let's go out.   **b.** Let's not go out.

(continued on next page)

3. A: It's late.

B: _____

    a. Let's go to bed.   **b.** Let's not go to bed.

4. A: The news isn't going to make your mother happy.

B: _____

    a. Let's tell her.   **b.** Let's not tell her.

5. A: We had a terrible meal at that restaurant last month.

B: _____

    a. Let's eat there.   **b.** Let's not eat there.

6. A: Here's a good movie.

B: _____

    a. Let's see it.   **b.** Let's not see it.

7. A: Miriam loves to read.

B: _____

    a. Let's buy her a book.   **b.** Let's not buy her a book.

❸ SUGGESTIONS WITH *WHY DON'T WE . . . ?*

Rewrite the sentences. Use **Why don't we . . . ?**

1. Let's finish class early today.

    Why don't we finish class early today? _____

2. Let's watch a movie in class today.

_____

3. Let's do less homework.

_____

4. Let's play more games in class.

_____

5. Let's have a party in class next week.

_____

6. Let's stop taking tests.

_____

4 SUGGESTIONS WITH *LET'S* . . . AND *WHY DON'T WE* . . . ?

What are the people saying? Complete the suggestions. Use the words in the box.

call and ask	~~have Chinese food~~	take a taxi
go skiing	~~invite a lot of~~ people	tell people

1. Mark and Kathy want to have a small wedding.

Let's __not invite a lot of people__.

2. Judy and Ken are thinking about where to go for dinner.

Why __don't we have Chinese food__?

3. Ari and Sylvia are talking about winter vacation plans.

Why _____?

4. Laura and Tony want to keep their engagement a secret.

Let's _____.

5. Mary and Bill are late for an appointment.

Let's _____.

6. Ana doesn't know if she and her friend can still get tickets for a concert.

Why _____?

5 EDITING

Correct the conversation. There are five mistakes. The first one is corrected for you.

A: It's Lisa's birthday tomorrow. ~~Let~~ Let's give her a gift.

B: That's a great idea. Why we don't give her some flowers?

A: No. Let's don't give her flowers. That's not very interesting.

(continued on next page)

B: Then how about a book? She likes to read. Let's us give her that new book by Sandy Morita.

A: I don't want to give her a book. Everybody gives her books.

B: Then why don't we take her out to a nice restaurant? She rarely goes out to eat.

A: Okay. Let's to take her to that Japanese restaurant near the park. She likes Japanese food a lot.

B: Good idea.

6 CONVERSATION COMPLETION

Complete the conversation. Use the words in the box. (Don't look at page 232 in your Student Book.)

contributions	How	~~look~~	that's
do	let's	not	truck
don't	Like	terrible	Why

MARK: Take a _____look_____ at this article.
1.

KATHY: _____ awful! They lost everything!
2.

MARK: It's _____, and I know Jon Somers. He
3.

drives a _____ for *The Seattle Daily*. A
4.

terrific guy! He's always there for others.

KATHY: Well, now let's _____ something for *him*.
5.

MARK: _____ what? He needs money. We _____ have money.
6. 7.

KATHY: No, but you're a journalist. Your words are powerful. And I can write too.

_____ don't we write an article about him for the paper? The paper can
8.

ask readers for _____.
9.

MARK: You know, _____ a wonderful idea.
10.

KATHY: Let's ask Steve to help.

MARK: Let's _____ ask Steve right away. First let's write the article.
11.

KATHY: Okay. So _____ get started.
12.

MARK: Now?

KATHY: Sure. There's no time like the present.

REQUESTS: *I WOULD LIKE . . . ;*
INVITATIONS: *WOULD YOU LIKE . . . ?*

1 SHORT ANSWERS TO POLITE INVITATIONS

Answer the questions. Use the answers in the box.

Yes, please.	Yes, I'd love to.
No, thank you.	Sorry, I can't.

1. Would you like some ice cream?

   Yes, please. (OR: No, thank you.)

2. Would you like to go to a party tonight?

   _____

3. Would you like to go to a museum on Sunday?

   _____

4. Would you like a cup of coffee?

   _____

5. Would you like to go fishing tomorrow?

   _____

6. Would you like a hamburger for dinner tonight?

   _____

7. Would you like some candy?

   _____

② LIKE VS. *WOULD LIKE*

Complete the conversations. Use **do** *or* **would**.

1. **A:** _____Would_____ you like some help?

   B: No, thanks. I'm okay.

2. **A:** _____ you like this book?

   B: It's okay.

3. **A:** _____ the kids like to play chess?

   B: I think so.

4. **A:** _____ you like a glass of water?

   B: Yes, please.

5. **A:** _____ you like to dance?

   B: Yes, I'd love to.

6. **A:** _____ you like fish?

   B: Not really.

7. **A:** _____ you like to go to a concert or see a play on Saturday night?

   B: Sorry, I can't. I'm busy on Saturday night.

③ AFFIRMATIVE STATEMENTS WITH *WOULD LIKE*

Rewrite the sentences. Use **'d like** *or* **would like**.

1. I want a cup of tea.

   I'd like a cup of tea.

2. We want to buy two tickets.

   _____

3. Do you want to go to the soccer game with me?

   _____

4. José wants some CDs for his birthday.

   _____

5. The children want some pizza.

_____

6. Do you and your friends want to have dinner with us?

_____

7. The teacher wants to talk to you.

_____

8. Do you want to go shopping with us?

_____

④ REQUESTS AND INVITATIONS WITH *WOULD LIKE*

Read the situations. What can you say? Write sentences. Use **'d like** *or* **would like**.

1. Invite someone to your birthday party next week.

   Would you like to come to my birthday party next week?

2. Tell your teacher you want to leave class early today.

   I'd like to leave class early today.

3. Tell a waiter that you want a bagel and some orange juice.

_____

4. Find out if your classmate wants a piece of chocolate.

_____

5. Invite your teacher to meet you and your classmates for dinner.

_____

6. Tell a friend you want to get a new car.

_____

7. Find out if your teacher wants something to eat from the school cafeteria.

_____

8. Invite a classmate to go for coffee after class.

_____

5 EDITING

Correct the conversation. There are seven mistakes. The first one is corrected for you.

A: So where~~you~~ ^{would} you like to go on our honeymoon?

B: I don't know. I like to go to a lot of different places.

A: Do you like to go somewhere far away, maybe to another country?

B: I'm not sure. I'd like going somewhere different, but we only have ten days.

A: Well, what about Mexico? That's not far away, and it's a different country.

B: Would you like Mexican food?

A: Oh, yeah. I like it a lot.

B: Okay. So where you'd like to go in Mexico? There are many interesting things to see.

A: I don't know. Why don't we talk to your friend, the travel agent?

B: Good idea. Would you like call now?

A: No. Let's do it tomorrow.

6 CONVERSATION COMPLETION

Complete the conversation. Use the words in the box. (Don't look at page 238 in your Student Book.)

are	guys	like	We'd
break	I'd	Sure	what
Do	Let's	~~This~~	Would

MICHELLE: Hello?

JEREMY: Hi, Michelle. _____This_____ is Jeremy.
                 1.

MICHELLE: Oh, hi, Jeremy!

JEREMY: Uh, . . . I was wondering . . . _____ you
                                        2.

        like to go out for pizza and then go ice skating?

        Kevin and Maria are going.

MICHELLE: Oh, _____ love to. When?
              3.

JEREMY: Saturday afternoon, about 4:30?

MICHELLE: Good. _____ you want to meet somewhere?
　　　　　　　　　　　4.

JEREMY: Yeah. _____ meet in front of the pizza place at 4:15.
　　　　　　　　　5.

MICHELLE: Sure. See you at 4:15 on Saturday. 'Bye.

JEREMY: 'Bye.

　　　　　　[Saturday]

WAITER: All right. What would you all _____?
　　　　　　　　　　　　　　　　　　6.

JEREMY: A large pizza. A supreme.

WAITER: And _____ would you like on the pizza?
　　　　　　　　7.

KEVIN: _____ like pepperoni and cheese. Okay,
　　　　　　8.

you _____?
　　　9.

MARIA: _____. But let's have anchovies, too.
　　　　　10.

KEVIN: Maria! Give me a _____! You're not
　　　　　　　　　　　　　　11.

serious, _____ you?
　　　　　　12.

MARIA: No! Just kidding. Actually, I hate anchovies.

NECESSITY: *MUST* AND *HAVE TO*

① **AFFIRMATIVE AND NEGATIVE STATEMENTS WITH *MUST* AND *HAVE TO***

True or false? Write **T** *or* **F**.

_____ 1. In my country, high school students have to wear a uniform.

_____ 2. They have to stand when the teacher enters the classroom.

_____ 3. They mustn't ask any questions.

_____ 4. They have to study a foreign language.

_____ 5. They don't have to study math.

_____ 6. They mustn't be late for class.

_____ 7. They don't have to listen to the teacher.

_____ 8. They have to do homework.

_____ 9. They mustn't talk during tests.

_____ 10. They don't have to take a lot of tests.

② **STATEMENTS WITH *HAVE TO***

Rewrite the sentences. Use **have to**, **has to**, **don't have to**, *or* **doesn't have to**.

1. It's necessary for the teacher to correct our homework.

   The teacher has to correct our homework.

2. It's not necessary for us to do all the exercises in this book.

   We don't have to do all the exercises in this book.

3. It's not necessary for the teacher to clean the room.

   _____

4. It's necessary for some students to do extra homework.

   _____

5. It's not necessary for me to sit near the board.

_____

6. It's necessary for us to speak English in class.

_____

7. It's necessary for me to bring my books to class.

_____

8. It's not necessary for the teacher to work during the school vacation.

_____

9. It's necessary for lunch to be at 12:00.

_____

3 STATEMENTS WITH *HAVE TO*

Complete the sentences. Use **have to** *or* **don't have to**.

1. Tennis players (play) _____ have to play _____ with a racquet.

2. Tennis players (be) _____ don't have to be _____ tall.

3. Tennis players (hit) _____ a ball.

4. Tennis players (move) _____ a lot.

5. Tennis players (wear) _____ a hat.

6. Soccer players (run) _____ a lot.

7. Soccer players (be) _____ fast.

8. Soccer players (use) _____ their feet a lot.

9. Soccer players (have) _____ special equipment except for a ball.

10. Soccer players (hit) _____ the ball with their heads.

4 AFFIRMATIVE AND NEGATIVE STATEMENTS WITH *MUST*

Look at the pictures. Write sentences. Use **must** *or* **mustn't** *and the words in parentheses.*

1. (talk)

People mustn't talk.

2. (have a ticket)

People must have a ticket.

3. (touch the paintings)

_____

4. (eat or drink)

_____

5. (be quiet)

_____

6. (write in the books)

_____

7. (wear a seat belt)

_____

8. (use cell phones)

_____

5 QUESTIONS WITH *HAVE TO*

Write questions. Use **have to**. *Then answer the questions.*

1. you / wash / your clothes

   Do you have to wash your clothes?   Yes, I do. (OR: No, I don't.)

2. what time / you / leave / home every day

   What time do you have to leave home every day?   At eight o'clock.

3. your mother / wash your clothes

4. what / you / do / at home

5. you / give / your parents money

6. your parents / give / you money

7. how many hours a week / your father / work

8. you / cook for yourself

6 EDITING

Correct the conversation. There are eight mistakes. The first one is corrected for you.

A: How's your new school? Do you ~~must~~ ^{have} to follow a lot of new rules?

B: Oh, yeah. The worst is that we must are there early—at 8:00 A.M. That means I have to leave home at 6:30, and my mother have to drive me. She's not happy.

A: Has she to pick you up?

B: No, she hasn't. I take the bus home. The good thing is that I mustn't wear a uniform to this school. I can wear jeans and a T-shirt.

A: What about homework? Do you have a lot?

B: Of course. And I don't have to forget it, or I have stay after school for two hours.

UNIT

38 ADVICE: *SHOULD / SHOULDN'T*

---

1 AFFIRMATIVE AND NEGATIVE STATEMENTS WITH *SHOULD*

Where are the people going? Use the words in the box.

the beach	an interview
a campsite	a wedding

sunscreen   flashlight

1. You should put on sunscreen. _____the beach_____

2. You should take a gift. _____

3. You should be on time. _____

4. You should take a flashlight. _____

5. You shouldn't stay in the sun all day. _____

6. You shouldn't look at your feet all the time. _____

7. You shouldn't say you didn't have a good time. _____

8. You shouldn't forget your sleeping bag. _____

② AFFIRMATIVE AND NEGATIVE STATEMENTS WITH *SHOULD*

Write sentences. Use **you should** *or* **you shouldn't** *and the words in parentheses.*

1. (smoke) __You shouldn't smoke._____

2. (drink / a lot of water) __You should drink a lot of water._____

3. (drink / a lot of soda) _____

4. (eat / a lot of ice cream) _____

5. (eat / a lot of fruit) _____

6. (brush / your teeth after every meal) _____

7. (exercise) _____

8. (sleep / only two or three hours a night) _____

③ SHOULD VS. HAVE TO

Complete the sentences. Use **should** *or* **have to**.

1. English teachers __have to__ know English.

   English teachers __should__ read a lot in English.

2. Doctors _____ study for many years.

   Doctors _____ be friendly.

3. Tour guides _____ speak other languages.

   Tour guides _____ know a lot about different places.

4. Nurses _____ help patients a lot.

   They often _____ work at night.

④ SHOULDN'T VS. DON'T HAVE TO

Complete the sentences. Use **shouldn't** *or* **don't have to**.

1. Teachers __don't have to__ cook meals for students.

   Teachers __shouldn't__ get angry at students.

(continued on next page)

2. Taxi drivers _____ talk on the phone and drive.

Taxi drivers _____ go to college.

3. Police officers _____ be athletic.

Police officers _____ be afraid to face dangerous situations.

4. Secretaries _____ be rude on the telephone.

Secretaries _____ stand up a lot.

⑤ STATEMENTS AND QUESTIONS WITH *SHOULD*

Complete the conversation. Use **should** *and the words in parentheses.*

AMANDA: Let's give a party for Kathy before the wedding.

MARIA: Who _____ should we invite _____?
1. (we / invite)

AMANDA: All of her girlfriends.

MARIA: _____ too?
2. (Mark / come)

AMANDA: No. The party's going to be for women only.

MARIA: Then _____ invitations to her mother and aunts?
3. (we / send)

AMANDA: Of course. Now what kind of food _____?
4. (there / be)

MARIA: That depends. _____ the party at home or at a
5. (we / have)

restaurant?

AMANDA: Oh. I think _____ the party at home. I can do it at
6. (we / have)

my place.

MARIA: Okay. Then I think _____ Kathy's favorite kinds
7. (we / serve)

of food.

AMANDA: That's fine, but _____ any difficult dishes. You know
8. (we / not make)

I'm a terrible cook.

MARIA: Don't worry. I'll do the cooking. When _____?
9. (the party / be)

AMANDA: How about two weeks before the wedding? And _____
10. (we / not say)

anything to Kathy. Let's make it a surprise.

MARIA: Okay. Good idea.

6 EDITING

Correct the conversations. There are six mistakes. The first one is corrected for you.

1. **A:** ~~Do I should~~ ^{Should I} take another English class?

   B: I think you do.

2. **A:** You should to try to speak English more.

   B: I know, but it's difficult.

3. **A:** The teacher doesn't like her job.

   B: She should gets another one.

4. **A:** You don't should sleep in class.

   B: I know. I should sleep more at night.

5. **A:** What we should study for the test?

   B: The last five units of the book.

7 CONVERSATION COMPLETION

Complete the conversation. Use the words in the box. (Don't look at page 250 in your Student Book.)

agree	guess	~~meet~~	should
don't	I'd	mind	too
graduate	It's	need	wondering

JUDY: Ken, here's someone you should

   _____meet_____.
            1.

KEN: Okay.

JUDY: Steve, _____ like to introduce
                         2.
   you to someone special.

STEVE: Sure, Judy.

JUDY: This is my brother, Ken. He's visiting from

   Michigan. He's on spring break now.

STEVE: _____ good to meet you, Ken.
              3.

(continued on next page)

KEN: Good to meet you _____.
                                        4.

JUDY: Steve, Ken has a question. You're a professor, so you're a good person to ask.

STEVE: Sure. What's on your _____?
                                              5.

KEN: I'm _____ about school. I'm going to _____ in a couple of
                    6.   **7.**
months. Should I go to college next fall or wait a year?

STEVE: Hmm. Big question. What do you want to study?

KEN: Well, that's just it. I don't know. I _____ I should go to college, but . . .
                                                          8.

STEVE: But?

KEN: I want to do something else for a while. Actually, I'd like to travel.

STEVE: Well, a lot of people don't _____ with this, but here's my opinion. I think
                                                    9.
kids _____ go to college when they're ready. So why _____
            10.   **11.**
you wait a year?

KEN: Hmm. I _____ to think about it. Thanks a lot, Steve.
                        12.

ANSWER KEY

Where the full form is given, the contraction is also acceptable. Where the contracted form is given, the full form is also acceptable, unless the exercise is about contractions.

PART | **IMPERATIVES AND PRONOUNS**

UNIT 1 IMPERATIVES

1

2. b   4. b   6. a
3. a   5. a

2

1. Close, Look at
2. Listen to, Look at
3. Look at, Read
4. Answer, Ask, Listen to, Look at
5. Ask, Listen to, Look at
6. Close

3

2. Five   5. eight   8. nine
3. seven   6. three   9. Six
4. ten   7. One   10. four

4

2. Hi. **I'm** Maria Sanchez.
3. How **are you**?
4. Sure. **Please sit** down.

5

2. Nice   5. nervous   8. how
3. I'm   6. Listen   9. Don't
4. teacher   7. tape   10. Bye.

UNIT 2 THIS IS / THESE ARE; SUBJECT PRONOUNS

1

2. f
3. d, e
4. g
5. h
6. i
7. a, b
8. h, i

2

3

2. It	5. She	8. It
3. I	6. He	9. We
4. It	7. They	10. They

4

2. This is Jackie Chan.
3. These are Prince William and Prince Harry.
4. This is Céline Dion.
5. These are Venus and Serena Williams.
6. These are Emperor Akihito and Empress Michiko.
7. This is Cameron Diaz.
8. This is Albert Einstein.
9. This is Louis Armstrong.

5

2. This is your book.
3. Is this your ticket?
4. These are your keys.
5. This is my house.
6. Is this your apartment?
7. Are these your friends?
8. These are your seats.

6

2. a	4. b	6. a
3. b	5. a	

7

2. **Are these** your keys?
3. **It** is big.
4. **These** are my books.
5. These are my **pets**.
6. Yes, her name is Mary. **She** is a teacher.

PART ‖ **THE VERB *BE*: PRESENT**

UNIT **THE PRESENT OF *BE*: STATEMENTS**

1

√ — 2, 4, 5, 8

2

3. isn't	5. is	7. isn't
4. isn't	6. is	8. is

3

2. is	6. are	10. am
3. is	7. are	11. is
4. is	8. are	
5. is	9. is	

4

2. It is beautiful.
3. She is not cold.
4. We are not on vacation.
5. They are nice.
6. You are not from here.

5

2. We're from Tokyo.
3. They aren't here. (OR They're not here.)
4. I'm not the teacher.
5. He's my cousin.
6. You aren't noisy. (OR You're not noisy.)

6

2. aren't (OR 're not), 're
3. isn't, 's
4. 's, isn't (OR 's not)
5. isn't (OR 's not), 's
6. 'm, 'm not

7

2. A: **Is** the food good?
   B: **It's** delicious.
3. A: This **is** my cousin.
   B: **Is** she a student?
4. A: **Are** you from Mexico?
   B: No, **we're** from Peru.
5. A: **Are** your cousins Amy and Mary here on vacation?
   B: No, **they're** here on business.

8

2. is	6. Australia	10. are
3. They're	7. opera	11. you
4. too	8. capital	12. am
5. not	9. We're	

UNIT 4 — THIS IS / THOSE ARE; POSSESSIVE ADJECTIVES; PLURAL NOUNS

❶

2. a   3. b   4. b

❷

2. Her name's
3. That's my father.
4. His name's

❸

2. That car is from Italy.
3. That child is from Canada.
4. That boy is from Egypt.
5. That dish is from Austria.

❹

2. Those people are from Mexico.
3. Those girls are from Japan.
4. Those glasses are from Australia.
5. Those computers are from the United States.

❺

2. my   5. His   8. Her
3. Their   6. Our
4. my   7. her

❻

2. b   4. a   6. a
3. a   5. b

❼

2. A: Are those **your** children?
   B: No, they're our **grandchildren**.
3. A: Are **those** your glasses?
   B: No, they're my **sunglasses**.
4. A: Those **people** are teachers.
   B: **Their** names are Steve Beck and Annie Macintosh.
5. A: **Is that** your granddaughter?
   B: Yes, **her** name's Jessica.

❽

2. My
3. her
4. their
5. Its
6. It's
7. grandchildren
8. granddaughter
9. that
10. grandson
11. His
12. He's

UNIT 5 — THE PRESENT OF BE: YES / NO QUESTIONS; QUESTIONS WITH WHO AND WHAT

❶

Conversation 1
B: Oh. She's my teacher. Her name's Amy.
A: What's her last name?
B: Diaz.
A: Is she friendly?
B: Yes, she is. She's very nice.

Conversation 2
B: No, that's my sister Kathy.
A: What does she do?
B: She's a writer.
A: Is she famous?
B: No, she isn't.

❷

(Answers will vary.)

❸

2. Is she your sister?
3. Are they from Peru?
4. Is he an actor?
5. Is it Woolson?
6. Are you Joe?
7. Are they here on business?

❹

2. Yes, I am. (OR No, I'm not.)
3. Yes, I am. (OR No, I'm not.)
4. Yes, she / he is. (OR No, she / he isn't. OR No, she's / he's not.)
5. Yes, she / he is. (OR No, she / he isn't. OR No, she's / he's not.)
6. Yes, it is. (OR No, it isn't. OR No, it's not.)
7. No, they aren't. (OR No, they're not.)
8. Yes, we are. (OR No, we aren't. OR No, we're not.)

5

2. Ben.
3. My grandchildren.
4. A key.

6

2. That's my brother.
3. It's Canberra.
4. It's Lynn Martin.

7

2. A: **Are** you and Joe married?
3. A: **Who's** that boy?
   B: **That's** my son.
4. A: **What's** the capital of the United States?
   B: **It's** Washington, D.C.
5. A: **Is** that woman your mother?
   B: Yes, **she is**.
6. A: **Is** Bob a travel agent?

8

2. you
3. it
4. Who's
5. Is
6. Yes
7. does
8. He's
9. Her
10. she
11. she's
12. What

UNIT 6 THE PRESENT OF *BE*: QUESTIONS WITH *WHERE*; PREPOSITIONS OF PLACE

1

2. supermarket, f
3. movie theater, e
4. library, d
5. restaurant, b
6. bank, a
7. art museum, h
8. post office, g
9. park, j
10. flower shop, l
11. gym, i
12. hospital, k

2

3. T
4. F
5. F
6. F
7. T
8. T

3

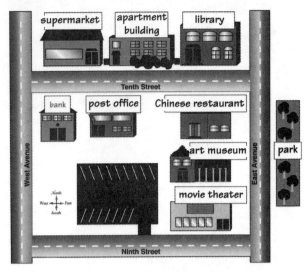

4

2. Where are Mr. and Mrs. Lin from?
3. Where are the doctors from?
4. Where's Paul from?
5. Where are you from?

5

2. seventh
3. third
4. tenth

6

2. 3rd
3. 1st
4. 2nd

7

2. It's on the first floor.
3. It's on the third floor.
4. It's on the fourth floor.
5. It's on the sixth floor.
6. It's on the second floor.

8

Hi Paula,

What's your phone number, and where's your apartment? Is it on Main Street?
And what floor is your apartment **on**?

Bob

Hi Bob,

My phone number **is** 555-0900. My apartment isn't **on** Main Street. It's **at** 212 Park Avenue. Take the number 12 bus. My apartment building is next **to** the post office, and my apartment is on the **ninth** floor.

Paula

PART ||| THE VERB *BE*: PAST

UNIT **7** THE PAST OF *BE*: STATEMENTS, *YES / NO* QUESTIONS

1

(Answers will vary.)

2

(Answers will vary.)

3

2. Kate wasn't in class yesterday.
3. I was happy yesterday.
4. It was cold yesterday.
5. The children were sad yesterday.
6. We weren't noisy yesterday.
7. The streets weren't crowded yesterday.
8. You were hot yesterday.
9. I wasn't alone yesterday.

4

2. wasn't	5. was	8. wasn't
3. was	6. was	9. were
4. were	7. weren't	

5

2. Were Tim and Jessica at a movie last night? Yes, they were.
3. Were Bill and Steve at a play yesterday? Yes, they were.
4. Was Judy at a party yesterday? Yes, she was.
5. Was Mark at home yesterday? No, he wasn't.
6. Were Mary, Annie, and Ben at a soccer game last night? No, they weren't.

6

1. B: Yes, they **were**.
2. A: Hi. **How's** it going?
3. A: **Was** the movie funny yesterday?
   B: No, it **wasn't**.
4. A: Where were you last night?
   B: **I** was at home.

7

2. How's	6. wasn't	10. great
3. last	7. movie	11. funny
4. weren't	8. alone	12. it
5. were	9. was	

UNIT THE PAST OF *BE*: *WH-* QUESTIONS

1

2. a	4. a	6. c
3. c	5. b	7. a

2

(Answers will vary.)

3

2. How was it?
3. Where were you?
4. Who was with you?
5. How long were you there?
6. How was the weather?

4

2. It was hot and rainy.
3. It was cold and sunny.
4. It was freezing and cloudy.
5. It was warm and sunny.
6. It was cool and windy.

5

2. **Where** were the students?
3. How long **was** class?
4. **It** was sunny and warm.
5. When **were** they here?
6. **What** movie was it?

6

2. you	8. was	
3. long	9. Who	
4. wonderful	10. Remember	
5. weather	11. guide	
6. cool	12. last	
7. Were		

PART IV THE PRESENT PROGRESSIVE

UNIT THE PRESENT PROGRESSIVE: STATEMENTS

❶

2. d	5. h	8. b
3. f	6. c	
4. g	7. a	

❷

2. closing	6. fixing	10. opening
3. doing	7. looking	11. running
4. dreaming	8. listening	12. shining
5. enjoying	9. moving	

❸

3. Tim's drinking. He isn't eating.
4. Judy isn't reading. She's talking.
5. Bill and Steve are listening. They aren't talking.
6. The athletes aren't playing basketball. They're playing soccer.
7. Mary, Annie, and Ben aren't sitting in the park. They're sitting in the living room.

❹

2. I'm (OR I'm not) wearing glasses right now.
3. I'm (OR I'm not) listening to music right now.
4. I'm (OR I'm not) sitting in my bedroom right now.
5. I'm (OR I'm not) eating right now.
6. I'm (OR I'm not) sitting with my friend right now.
7. I'm (OR I'm not) drinking water right now.
8. I'm (OR I'm not) looking at a computer right now.

❺

Hello from Seattle. It's raining right now, but **we're having** fun. Jenny and I are **sitting** in a restaurant. **I'm** eating lunch. The food here in Seattle is good. **Jenny's not** eating. **She's drinking** coffee. We aren't **talking**. Jenny's **reading** the newspaper.

❻

2. I'm	6. is	10. not
3. are	7. They're	11. She
4. I	8. was	12. She's
5. wearing	9. fun	

UNIT 10 THE PRESENT PROGRESSIVE: YES / NO QUESTIONS

❶

2. Yes, it is. (OR No, it isn't.)
3. Yes, I am. (OR No, I'm not.)
4. Yes, she / he is. (OR No, she / he isn't.)
5. Yes, they are. (OR No, they aren't.)
6. Yes, I am. (OR No, I'm not.)
7. Yes, I am. (OR No, I'm not.)
8. Yes, it is. (OR No, it isn't.)

❷

2. Is he sleeping in his bedroom?
3. Are they writing a letter?
4. Is Ben doing his homework alone?
5. Are you talking to your boss?
6. Is Kelly daydreaming about her vacation?
7. Are the kids cleaning the bathroom?
8. Are you baking cookies?

❸

3. Are Jessica and Tim eating at a restaurant? No, they aren't.
4. Is the cat wearing a hat? Yes, it is.
5. Are Ben and Annie playing cards? Yes, they are.
6. Is Jeremy playing a computer game? No, he isn't.
7. Is Tim writing a letter? Yes, he is.
8. Is the cat sitting on the chair? Yes, it is.
9. Is the cat babysitting? No, it isn't.

❹

2. He's making
3. Are your parents eating
4. My parents are having dinner
5. Is he sleeping
6. He's doing

❺

1. B: No, **I'm** not.
2. A: **Is** the teacher asking a question?
   B: Yes, **she is**.
3. A: Is Mr. Olson **working**?
   B: No, he isn't. He's **eating** lunch.
4. A: Is **Kelly babysitting**?
   B: No, she's not. **She's** watching a video with her friend.
5. A: **Are** Tim and his boss wearing suits?
   B: Yes, **they are**.

6

2. listening
3. Everything's
4. doing
5. baking
6. homework
7. sleeping
8. are
9. having
10. cool
11. anniversary
12. See

UNIT 11 THE PRESENT PROGRESSIVE: *WH-* QUESTIONS

1

2. Who
3. What
4. Where
5. Why
6. How
7. What
8. Who
9. Why

2

2. Where is Tim barbecuing hot dogs? In the park.
3. Why are the Olsons eating in the park? Because they're having a picnic.
4. What are the children playing? Soccer.
5. Where is Jessica sitting? At a table.
6. Why is Tim wearing an apron? Because he's cooking.
7. How is the picnic going? Great.
8. Who is playing soccer with the children? Jeremy is.
9. What are Judy and her friends doing? They're listening to the radio.

3

2. Who are you talking
3. What are they baking?
4. Who's watching
5. Where's he studying?

4

2. A: What **are** the people watching?
3. A: Why **is Mark** wearing a suit?
   B: Because **he's** going to a wedding.
4. A: **How's** everything going?
   B: Great. **We're having** a lot of fun.
5. A: Where **are** Ben and Annie going?
6. A: Who's Jeremy **sending** an e-mail message to?

5

2. Where's
3. Why
4. out
5. What's
6. Broccoli
7. on
8. I'm
9. Who
10. What
11. starved
12. Apple pie with ice cream

PART V THE SIMPLE PRESENT

UNIT 12 THE SIMPLE PRESENT: STATEMENTS

1

3. T
4. T
5. T
6. T
7. F
8. T
9. F

2

2. reports
3. teaches
4. act
5. babysits
6. sings
7. play

3

2. doesn't have
3. don't speak
4. don't need
5. don't like
6. doesn't want
7. don't have
8. doesn't teach
9. doesn't rain

4

2. I like (OR I don't like) broccoli.
3. I like (OR I don't like) spaghetti.
4. I like (OR I don't like) apple pie.
5. I like (OR I don't like) ice cream.
6. I like (OR I don't like) pizza.

5

2. look
3. don't look
4. have
5. has
6. work
7. works
8. work
9. doesn't work
10. goes
11. fixes
12. loves
13. doesn't love
14. speak
15. don't speak
16. speak
17. don't come
18. comes
19. comes
20. speaks
21. doesn't speak

6

My brother, Ken, **lives** with my parents. They **live** in a big house. My father **has** a new car. He cleans his car every day. Ken **doesn't** have a new car. His car is old. It **doesn't** run, but he **loves** it. My mother **doesn't** love cars. She **loves** her garden. She **works** in it every Saturday and Sunday. I **don't** see my family often, but we talk on the weekend.

7

2. go	**6.** eyes	**10.** watch
3. lives	**7.** likes	**11.** goes
4. look	**8.** don't	**12.** sounds
5. hair	**9.** doesn't	

UNIT 13 THE SIMPLE PRESENT:
YES / NO QUESTIONS

1

3. J	**6.** A	**9.** J
4. A	**7.** A	**10.** A
5. J	**8.** J	

2

2. f	**4.** c	**6.** e
3. b	**5.** a	

3

3. No, she doesn't.
4. No, they don't.
5. No, she doesn't.
6. Yes, they do.
7. Yes, she does.
8. Yes, I do. (OR No, I don't.)
9. Yes, I do. (OR No, I don't.)

4

2. Does she work on Sunday?
3. Does he speak Japanese?
4. Do they have a cat?
5. Does she know Kathy?
6. Do they need a new radio?
7. Does it have a gym?
8. Do you speak Portuguese at home?

5

2. Are, Do	**4.** Are, Do	**6.** Are, Do
3. Do, Is	**5.** Do, Does	**7.** Is, Does

6

2. Does he like
3. Does your brother wear
4. That's
5. Do you like
6. I love
7. Jeremy doesn't like
8. Do you have
9. Jeremy loves

7

2. A: Does your grandmother **knit**?
   B: Yes, she **does**.
3. A: **Do** your three friends play basketball?
   B: One friend **plays** basketball. The other two play soccer.
4. A: **Does** *Focus on Grammar* have a lot of grammar practice?
   B: Yes, it **does**.
5. B: No, we don't.

UNIT 14 THE SIMPLE PRESENT:
WH- QUESTIONS

1

2. g	**5.** b	**8.** c
3. f	**6.** h	
4. e	**7.** a	

2

2. goes to school
3. do you get to school
4. do you do
5. does he go to school early
6. does she go home for lunch
7. do you play games in class

3

2. It's twenty after seven.
3. It's twenty-five after seven.
4. It's twenty to eight.
5. It's ten to eight.
6. It's five to eight.
7. It's eleven o'clock.
8. It's one-thirty. (OR It's half past one.)
9. It's a quarter after two.
10. It's a quarter to seven.
11. It's twenty-five after ten.
12. It's twenty-five to four.

❹

2. What does that store sell?
3. Why do you knit sweaters?
4. What colors do you like?
5. Who likes chocolate?
6. Where do your cousins live?
7. What does your father do?

❺

YUKO: What time does English class start?
OMAR: At 1:00.
YUKO: What time **does** class finish?
OMAR: At 2:30.
YUKO: What **does** *dislike* mean?
OMAR: It means "not like."
YUKO: How **do** you say this word?
OMAR: I don't know.
YUKO: **Does** the teacher teach every day?
OMAR: No. She doesn't teach on Friday.
YUKO: What **do** we have for homework?
OMAR: Page 97.
YUKO: Why does Elena know all the answers?
OMAR: She **studies** a lot.

❻

2. mean
3. early
4. time
5. quarter
6. Where
7. ticket agent
8. late
9. else
10. cooking
11. What
12. Talking

UNIT 15 THE SIMPLE PRESENT: *BE* AND *HAVE*

❶

2. Vic
3. Sue
4. Sue
5. Vic
6. Tom
7. Sue
8. Tom
9. Sue
10. Tom

❷

(Answers will vary.)

❸

2. is
3. is
4. isn't
5. is
6. is
7. has
8. doesn't have
9. is
10. have
11. have
12. are

❹

3. What's the name of Bono's band?
4. Is Bono a violinist?
5. What's Bono's real name?
6. Where's he from?
7. Does he have any brothers or sisters?
8. Is he married?
9. Do they have children?
10. Where do they have a home?

❺

A: What's your name?
B: Alice.
A: How old **are** you?
B: I **am** twenty-four.
A: **Do** you have a big family?
B: Yes, I do. I have three sisters and four brothers.
A: Where do you live?
B: My home **is** near here. It's on Center Street.
A: Is **it** big?
B: No. **It's** small. I live alone. My family lives in another city.
A: **Do** you have a job?
B: No. I study at a university.

❻

2. isn't
3. is
4. like
5. He's
6. has
7. He
8. have
9. does
10. think
11. was
12. That's

UNIT 16 ADVERBS OF FREQUENCY

❶

(Answers will vary.)

❷

2. Steve does not exercise often.
3. Bill rarely eats at a restaurant.
4. It sometimes snows here.
5. Mary is not usually busy.
6. It is often hot in Cairo.

3

3. I sometimes play soccer.
4. Jessica often cooks dinner.
5. I am rarely late for class.
6. The food at that restaurant is never good.
7. Annie and Ben always start school at 8:30.
8. Josh often goes to the gym.
9. The park is sometimes crowded.
10. Robert rarely goes to the movies.

4

3. Do your children ever stay home alone?
4. How often do you listen to the radio?
5. Do you ever smoke?
6. How often does Tim cook dinner?
7. Are you ever busy on the weekend?

5

   Here is my schedule. I am usually busy on Monday evenings. I **often go** to the gym, or I play basketball. (Do you **ever play** basketball?) On Fridays I **always exercise** too. I go dancing! On Wednesdays and Thursdays I sometimes work late, but I'm often free on Tuesdays. I **usually finish** work at 5:30. Do you want to meet at Vincenzo's Italian Restaurant at 6:30? The food there is **always good**.

6

2. energy	6. Sometimes	10. enough
3. sleep	7. hurry	11. often
4. hours	8. breakfast	12. times
5. ever	9. always	

PART VI NOUNS, ARTICLES, AND CAN / CAN'T

UNIT 17 POSSESSIVE NOUNS; THIS / THAT / THESE / THOSE

2. What are those?
3. What's this?
4. What's that?

2. birds, 2
3. paper bag, 4
4. suspenders, 1

3

2. Amy's	4. Ari's
3. Renee's	5. Juan's

4

2. His parents' names are Jessica and Tim.
3. Steve's apartment is in Seattle.
4. The students' chairs are between the board and the window.
5. The teacher's desk is near the door.
6. Our daughters' husbands are very nice.
7. The children's room is on the second floor.
8. My friend's grandchildren visit her often.

5

2. Who is wearing Mara's jacket?
3. That is not Judy's backpack.
4. The baby is not sleeping
5. What is Steve's last name?
6. Amanda is here.
7. Where is the car?

6

2. A: The **women's** restroom is over there.
3. A: Who's **that** over there?
4. B: No. He's wearing his **brother's** tie. And **that** isn't Ken's sports jacket either.
5. B: Yeah. I like **Rose's** earrings too.

7

2. parents	6. They're	10. yours
3. parents'	7. this	11. that
4. brother's	8. these	12. Kathy's
5. those	9. Steve's	

UNIT 18 COUNT AND NON-COUNT NOUNS; SOME AND ANY

3. a	11. some	19. some
4. some	12. some	20. some
5. a	13. an	21. a
6. some	14. an	22. some
7. an	15. a	23. some
8. some	16. some	24. some
9. a	17. some	
10. some	18. a	

2

3. I don't have any oranges.
4. Eat some eggs.
5. We need some sandwiches.
6. She wants some olives.
7. Do you need any strawberries?

3

2. bottle, glass
3. bag, cup
4. slice
5. bag, bowl, cup

4

3. is	5. are	7. are
4. is	6. is	8. is

5

3. any	7. any	11. any
4. a	8. an	12. some
5. an	9. any	
6. some	10. some	

6

JOSH: Waiter? Excuse me. Can I have a glass of water, please?
WAITER: Sure. Ma'am, do you want **any** water?
JUDY: Yes, thank you.
WAITER: Here is your water. What would you like to eat?
JUDY: I'd like **a** sandwich and some iced tea. Oh, and **a** bowl of chocolate ice cream too.
WAITER: And you, sir?
JOSH: Tell me. **Is** the spaghetti here good?
WAITER: Yes, delicious.
JOSH: Okay. I'd like **some** spaghetti.
WAITER: And what about something to drink?
JOSH: I just want **this** water.

7

2. cup	6. on	10. an
3. all	7. bowl	11. strawberries
4. in	8. some	12. glass
5. at	9. fruit	

UNIT 19 *A / An* AND *THE; ONE / ONES*

1

2. e	4. c	6. a
3. b	5. d	

2

2. I like the formal ones. (OR I like the casual ones.)
3. I like the new one. (OR I like the old one.)
4. I like the black ones. (OR I like the white ones.)

3

3. –	6. the	9. –
4. the	7. –	10. –
5. the	8. the	

4

3. –	7. –	11. a
4. –	8. The	12. an
5. –	9. a	
6. The	10. a	

5

2. **B:** I like Chinese food.
3. **B:** No, I usually wear the gray **ones**.
4. **A:** Do you wear **a** tie to work?
   B: No, I don't like ties.
5. **A:** Do you have **a** white blazer?
6. **A:** Do you want **an** umbrella?
   B: No, I never use umbrellas.

6

2. a	6. size	10. one
3. an	7. the	11. ones
4. in	8. on	12. up
5. sale	9. look	

UNIT 20 CAN / CAN'T

①

1. In a kitchen, we can bake, cook, listen to the radio, and sit.
   We can't play golf, run, sleep, or swim.
2. At a beach, we can listen to the radio, run, sit, sleep, and swim.
   We can't bake, cook, or play golf.
3. In a hospital, we can listen to the radio, sit, and sleep.
   We can't bake, cook, play golf, run, or swim.
4. *(Answers will vary.)*

②

2. Can you give Kathy this message, please?
3. Can you tell me the answers, please?
4. Can you call the police, please?
5. Can you wait for me, please?
6. Can you help me with my homework, please?

③

3. can't water ski, can ski
4. can't play the guitar, can't play the piano
5. can swim, can dive
6. can swim, can't dive
7. can't water ski, can't ski
8. can play the guitar, can't play the piano
9. *(Answers will vary.)*
10. *(Answers will vary.)*

④

2. Can your teacher speak Spanish? Yes, she / he can. (OR No, she / he can't.)
3. Can your friends play soccer? Yes, they can. (OR No, they can't.)
4. Can you drive? Yes, I can. (OR No, I can't.)
5. Can your parents speak English? Yes, they can. (OR No, they can't.)
6. Can your father cook? Yes, he can. (OR No, he can't.)
7. Can you sing well? Yes, I can. (OR No, I can't.)
8. Can your mother play golf? Yes, she can. (OR No, she can't.)

⑤

2. How can I learn your language? *(Answers will vary.)*
3. Who can change American dollars? *(Answers will vary.)*
4. Where can I buy CDs? *(Answers will vary.)*
5. What can I do on the weekend in your town? *(Answers will vary.)*

⑥

A: I have a problem. Can you help me?
B: Sure. How **can** I help?
A: I **can't** understand the homework. Can you understand it?
B: Yes, I **can**. But I **can't explain** it well. **Can** the teacher explain it to you?
A: I **can't find** him.
B: He's in his office. I'm sure he **can help** you.

PART VII REVIEW OF THE PRESENT; THE SIMPLE PAST

UNIT 21 REVIEW: IMPERATIVE, PRESENT PROGRESSIVE, AND SIMPLE PRESENT

①

3. Yes, I do. (OR No, I don't.)
4. Yes, she / he does.
   (OR No, she / he doesn't.)
5. Yes, she / he is. (OR No, she / he isn't.)
6. Yes, they are. (OR No, they aren't.)
7. Yes, I do. (OR No, I don't.)
8. Yes, it does. (OR No, it doesn't.)
9. Yes, it is. (OR No, it isn't.)
10. Yes, I am. (OR No, I'm not.)

②

3. Don't speak
4. Speak
5. Do
6. Don't be

③

2. is playing, loves
3. is playing, doesn't play
4. speaks, are talking
5. goes, is diving
6. are playing, plays

④

2. I don't think
3. does this backpack belong
4. It's
5. is he
6. He's talking
7. are they talking
8. He has
9. I know
10. He doesn't look

5

1. B: **I go** to English class.
2. B: Yes, **I'm eating**.
3. B: **Open** the window.
4. A: **Do you want** a cup of coffee right now?
   B: Yes, please. I **need** a break.
5. A: Please **don't talk**. **You're** in a library.
6. A: I **like** your cousin. Introduce me to him.
   B: You can't talk to him in English. He **doesn't speak** English.

6

2. She's
3. Is
4. standing
5. Go
6. Show
7. I'm
8. need
9. Introduce
10. do
11. are
12. Don't

UNIT 22 THE SIMPLE PAST: REGULAR VERBS (STATEMENTS)

1

(Answers will vary.)

2

2. watched
3. listened
4. baked
5. visited
6. played

3

3. arrived
4. didn't cook
5. enjoyed
6. studied
7. called
8. asked
9. didn't want
10. didn't need

4

3. last month
4. two months ago
5. seven months ago
6. yesterday
7. two weeks ago
8. last night
9. yesterday morning
10. ten months ago

5

2. didn't watch
3. didn't talk
4. didn't enjoy
5. didn't play
6. didn't learn

6

2. didn't work
3. arrived
4. didn't look
5. didn't start
6. finished
7. didn't complain
8. wanted

7

Thanks for dinner last week. I **enjoyed** it very much. I hope I **didn't** talk a lot. I **liked** your kids a lot. Jeremy **showed** me some great computer games.

I talked to Rita's secretary again yesterday, but Rita didn't **return** my call.

Herb

PS Sorry I didn't **thank** you before, but I was very busy.

UNIT 23 THE SIMPLE PAST: REGULAR AND IRREGULAR VERBS

1

3. come, irregular verb
4. leave, irregular verb
5. see, irregular verb
6. play, regular verb
7. enjoy, regular verb
8. be, irregular verb
9. eat, irregular verb
10. like, regular verb
11. talk, regular verb
12. have, irregular verb
13. end, regular verb
14. get, irregular verb

2

2. I drank tea, but I didn't drink coffee.
3. I took a bus to class, but I didn't take a train.
4. I ate lunch in the school cafeteria, but I didn't eat in a restaurant.
5. We had homework, but we didn't have a lot of homework.
6. The teacher put the answers on the board, but he didn't put all the answers.
7. I went to the library after class, but I didn't go with friends.
8. I saw some classmates at the library, but I didn't see the teacher.

3

2. took (OR didn't take)
3. slept (OR didn't sleep)
4. came (OR didn't come)
5. bought (OR didn't buy)
6. went (OR didn't go)

4

2. Did the teacher drink coffee in class yesterday?
   Yes, she / he did. (OR No, she / he didn't.)
3. Did you and your friends go to the movies yesterday?
   Yes, we did. (OR No, we didn't.)
4. Did you eat breakfast yesterday?
   Yes, I did. (OR No, I didn't.)
5. Did you take a taxi yesterday?
   Yes, I did. (OR No, I didn't.)
6. Did your friends come to your home yesterday?
   Yes, they did. (OR No, they didn't.)
7. Did you buy ice cream yesterday?
   Yes, I did. (OR No, I didn't.)

5

1. **B:** No, I **didn't**.
2. **A:** I **went** on a picnic last Saturday.
3. **B:** No, and we **didn't drink** anything either.
4. **A:** I **didn't see** my keys on the table.
   B: We **put** them in your bag.
5. **A:** Did you **go** to school yesterday?
   B: Yes, I **did**.

6

2. called
3. went
4. snow
5. you
6. Did
7. ate
8. drank
9. Was
10. didn't
11. happened
12. you're

UNIT 24 THE SIMPLE PAST: WH- QUESTIONS

1

2. e
3. f
4. a
5. g
6. d
7. b

2

2. stopped
3. was
4. hit
5. got
6. stopped
7. had
8. broke
9. took
10. wasn't

3

2. When did the accident happen?
3. Who stopped at a green light?
4. Why did he stop?
5. Who hit the BMW?
6. Why did the driver of the white Toyota get angry at?
7. Who did the driver of the white Toyota get angry at?
8. What did they have?
9. Who had a fight?
10. Who broke up the fight?
11. Where did the woman take the driver of the BMW?
12. Who took the driver of the BMW to the hospital?

4

2. Where did you go on the weekend? (*Answers will vary.*)
3. What did you do last night? (*Answers will vary.*)
4. Who did you talk to yesterday? (*Answers will vary.*)
5. What did you have for homework last week? (*Answers will vary.*)

5

2. **A:** Who **built** your house?
   B: My grandfather **built** it.
3. **A:** Why did you **get** a letter from Steven Spielberg?
   B: Because I **wrote** him and he answered my letter.
4. **B:** The other team **won**.
5. **A:** What time **did** the game **begin**?
6. **A:** How **was** the party?

6

2. you weren't
3. did you go
4. We went
5. Did you stay
6. We spent
7. We flew
8. came
9. did you do
10. we stayed
11. talked
12. did you talk
13. I learned
14. Mark did
15. Did you meet
16. they had
17. came
18. did you meet
19. Was it
20. I enjoyed

PART VIII PRONOUNS, QUANTITY EXPRESSIONS, *THERE IS / THERE ARE*

UNIT 25 SUBJECT AND OBJECT PRONOUNS

1

2. They need a ride.
3. We want to go to the party.
4. It is small.
5. He invited a lot of people.
6. She didn't go to the party.

2

2. I met her.
3. I talked to them.
4. I didn't see them.
5. They put it outside all night.
6. Bill talked to us.

3

2. him	5. it	8. us
3. me	6. her	
4. them	7. them	

4

2. A: She loves you.
   B: I don't love her.
3. A: Can he give you the keys?
   B: He can't find them.
4. A: Can I help you?
   B: Can you show me your jackets?
5. A: Are these seats for us?
   B: No, they are for them.

5

2. them, They, She
3. him, he
4. it, me
5. it, It
6. you, you, he
7. her, she
8. us, them

6

Dear Anne,

Thank you for inviting us to the party. The children and **I** had a great time. The games were great. The kids loved **them**.

Did Bob and Sally find the gifts? I left **them** in their room. Did Bob like the tennis racquet? I bought it at Central Sports for **him**. I got Sally's soccer ball there too. Does **she** still play soccer? (I know you said, "No gifts," but what's a birthday without gifts?)

Why don't **we** meet one day for lunch? Give **me** a call.

Talk to you soon,
Sarah

7

2. him	6. your	10. us
3. so	7. them	11. me
4. to	8. He	12. you
5. her	9. I	

UNIT 26 HOW MUCH / HOW MANY

1

2. How many oranges does Steve have? Not many.
3. How many bananas does Steve have? Not many.
4. How much milk does Steve have? A lot.
5. How many apples does Steve have? A lot.
6. How much fruit does Steve have? A lot.
7. How much soda does Steve have? Not much.
8. How much yogurt does Steve have? Not much.
9. How much juice does Steve have? A lot.
10. How many eggs does Steve have? Not many.

2

(Answers will vary.)

3

3. many	6. a few	9. many
4. much	7. a little	10. much
5. a little	8. a few	

4

A: How much time do you get for vacation?
B: Four weeks.
A: Do you spend **a lot** of time at home during your vacation?
B: No, only a **few** days.
A: Where do you usually go?
B: We spend **a little** time at my wife's parents' home. Then we go to the beach. We spend some time with our friends there.
A: How many **friends** do you see at the beach?
B: Not **many**. Four or five.

5

2. many	6. was	10. did
3. were	7. a	11. nothing
4. time	8. people	12. way
5. much	9. bet	

UNIT 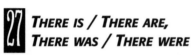 **27** *THERE IS / THERE ARE, THERE WAS / THERE WERE*

1

3. is	7. are	11. are
4. isn't	8. is	12. aren't
5. aren't	9. is	
6. is	10. isn't	

2

3. There is a television in my bedroom.
   (OR There isn't a television in my bedroom.)
4. There is a computer in my bedroom.
   (OR There isn't a computer in my bedroom.)
5. There is some food in my bedroom.
   (OR There isn't any food in my bedroom.)
6. There are some clothes in my bedroom.
   (OR There aren't any clothes in my bedroom.)
7. There are some shoes in my bedroom.
   (OR There aren't any shoes in my bedroom.)
8. There is a radio in my bedroom.
   (OR There isn't a radio in my bedroom.)
9. There are some books in my bedroom.
   (OR There aren't any books in my bedroom.)
10. There is some money in my bedroom.
    (OR There isn't any money in my bedroom.)

3

2. Are there any women in the picture? Yes, there are.
3. Are there any children in the picture? No, there aren't.
4. Is there any food in the picture? Yes, there is.
5. Are there any drinks in the picture? Yes, there are.
6. Is there a television in the picture? Yes, there is.
7. Is there a computer in the picture? No, there isn't.
8. Is there any furniture in the picture? Yes, there is.
9. Is there a car in the picture? No, there isn't.
10. Are there any books in the picture? No, there aren't.

4

2. There was	7. there were	10. there wasn't
3. there was	8. were there	11. There was
4. Was there	9. There weren't	12. there was
5. there was		
6. Were there		

5

There was a big fire last night. **It** was at Eighth and Center Streets. Years ago it was an apartment building, but there **aren't** any apartments there now. That's why last night there **were** no people in the building. Nobody knows how the fire started. **There** are many questions, but there **aren't** any answers yet.

6

2. did	6. there	10. were
3. went	7. was	11. are
4. cars	8. programs	12. They're
5. it	9. wasn't	

PART IX ADJECTIVES AND PREPOSITIONS

UNIT 28 DESCRIPTIVE ADJECTIVES

1

2

2. Why do you like serious women?
3. I want an athletic man.
4. That man is very generous.
5. They are talking to an interesting woman.
6. They are a happy couple.
7. Do you know any good-looking men?
8. His personal ad wasn't honest or funny.
   (OR funny or honest)

3

2. Venus and Serena Williams are famous tennis players.
3. Jessica and Tim live in a big house.
4. Josh and Amanda ate at an awful restaurant.
5. Judy likes sad movies.
6. Buy this cool CD player.
7. Jeremy bought an expensive CD player.
8. Bill and Mark have important jobs.

4

2. They are interesting men.
3. The black dogs are friendly.
4. The expensive cars are over there.
5. The artistic students are young Italians.
6. The boring books have a red cover.
7. The good-looking actors are from China.

5

2. Beijing and Mexico City are big cities.
3. Ferraris and BMWs are expensive cars.
4. Prince Harry and Prince William are young men.
5. Quebec is a small city.
6. Sushi is Japanese food.
7. The Beatles were British singers.
8. The Bible is an old book.
9. Van Gogh was a poor artist.

6

A: Where were you last night?
B: I had a date.
A: Really?
B: Yeah. I met a beautiful woman through a personal ad.
A: Oh, yeah? Tell me about her. Is she **athletic** like you?
B: Yeah. She plays three **different** sports.
A: What else?
B: Well, she's a **very funny person**, and she listens to **old** songs like me.
A: Does she work?
B: Yeah. She has **an** interesting job with a music company.
A: She sounds like she's the **perfect woman** for you.
B: She is.

UNIT 29 COMPARATIVE ADJECTIVES

1

2. cheap	5. hot	8. tall
3. dirty	6. large	9. good
4. easy	7. quick	10. bad

❷

One Syllable	Two Syllables Ending in —y	Two Syllables Not Ending in —y	More Than Two Syllables
cold dark old short warm	busy friendly funny healthy	active boring honest	artistic difficult exciting expensive important interesting

❸

2. busier
3. more difficult
4. shorter
5. funnier
6. better
7. more boring
8. more active
9. worse
10. colder

❹

2. hotter than
3. harder than (OR easier than)
4. older than
5. better than
6. more crowded than
7. longer than
8. worse than

❺

2. Which is easier, swimming or water skiing? Swimming.
3. Which are faster, planes or trains? Planes.
4. Which is warmer, January or July? *(Answer will vary.)*
5. Which is more popular around the world, soccer or baseball? Soccer.
6. Which is better for you, cake or fruit? Fruit.

❻

A: So how's your new apartment? Is it better than your old one?
B: Yes, it is. It's **bigger** and **cheaper**.
A: And where is it? Is the location good?
B: Oh, yeah. It's near the train station, so it's **easier** to get to work. And I like the neighborhood too. It has a lot of trees and is **more beautiful**. The neighborhood is also **cleaner**.
A: How many bedrooms are there?
B: Well, there are three bedrooms. One bedroom is smaller **than** the other two. It's **noisier** too. But the rest of the apartment is perfect. Why don't you come and see it this weekend?
A: That sounds like a good idea.

❼

2. got
3. real
4. worse
5. better
6. older
7. food
8. than
9. cheaper
10. entertainment
11. of
12. more

UNIT **SUPERLATIVE ADJECTIVES**

❶

2. worse, the worst
3. bigger, the biggest
4. more boring, the most boring
5. busier, the busiest
6. cleaner, the cleanest
7. more difficult, the most difficult
8. easier, the easiest
9. better, the best
10. healthier, the healthiest
11. more honest, the most honest
12. hotter, the hottest
13. more intelligent, the most intelligent
14. more popular, the most popular

❷

2. The Mercedes E500 is the most expensive car.
3. The Lincoln Navigator is the largest car.
4. Quebec is the coldest city.
5. New York is the largest city.
6. Istanbul is the oldest city.
7. Cheetahs are the fastest animal.
8. Lions are the most dangerous animal.
9. Elephants are the heaviest animal.
10. Andy Warhol was the most artistic person.
11. Princess Diana was the prettiest person.
12. Mother Teresa was the poorest person.

❸

(All answers to the questions will vary.)
2. What's the most expensive restaurant in your town?
3. What's the worst month for a vacation?
4. Who's the tallest person in your class?
5. Who's the youngest person in your class?
6. Who's the most popular singer in your country?
7. What's the funniest program on TV?
8. What's the coldest month of the year?
9. Who's the most beautiful actress in your country?

4

I like my class. I have the best teacher in the school, but our class is in the **worst** room. Last year I was in the largest room. Now I'm in **the** smallest.

There are ten students in the class. The nicest is Ram. He's really friendly. The **funniest** is Elisa. The **most intelligent** is Songkit, and the most artistic is Carlos.

We do lots of different things in class. The **most** interesting activities are the group discussions. The **most boring** part of the class is the homework. I really don't like homework.

5

2. strange
3. strangest
4. of
5. the
6. quickest
7. best
8. scooter
9. most
10. in
11. way
12. on

UNIT **PREPOSITIONS OF TIME:** *IN, ON, AT*

1

AT	IN	ON
four o'clock half past eleven night a quarter after two	April the evening May the morning 1990	June 1st November 3rd Thursday Tuesday weekdays the weekend

2

2. It's February second.
3. It's April thirtieth.
4. It's December thirty-first.
5. It's September first.
6. It's January third.
7. It's August ninth.
8. It's November eleventh.
9. It's March twenty-fifth.

3

2. on
3. on
4. on
5. on
6. on
7. on
8. at
9. in
10. at
11. in
12. at
13. at
14. at

4

(Answers will vary.)

5

2. **A:** Is your birthday **in** May?
3. **A:** Do you ever work **at** night?
   B: Sometimes. But I usually work **in** the morning and afternoon.
4. **B:** It's **at** five o'clock **in** the morning.
5. **A:** What do you do **on** weekends?
   B: **On** Sundays I go to my grandparents' home for dinner.

6

2. in
3. doing
4. fun
5. Saturday
6. afternoon
7. back
8. on
9. two-story
10. yourselves
11. looking
12. at

PART **THE FUTURE WITH *BE GOING TO***

UNIT **THE FUTURE WITH *BE GOING TO*: STATEMENTS**

1

2. b
3. b
4. b
5. a
6. b

2

2. They're going to see a movie.
3. She's going to sleep.
4. He's going to have lunch.
5. They're going to buy some food.
6. He's going to teach.
7. She's going to exercise.

❸

2. I'm not going to spend a lot of money this week.
3. We're not going to be absent from class this week.
4. He's not going to go on a class trip with his students this week.
5. They're not going to get married this week.
6. He's not going to take a test this week.
7. She's not going to have a party this week.

❹

2. I'm (OR I'm not) going to eat out next weekend.
3. I'm (OR I'm not) going to go out with friends next weekend.
4. I'm (OR I'm not) going to go shopping next weekend.
5. I'm (OR I'm not) going to the movies next weekend.
6. I'm (OR I'm not) going to play soccer next weekend.
7. I'm (OR I'm not) going to study next weekend.
8. I'm (OR I'm not) going to visit relatives next weekend.
9. I'm (OR I'm not) going to wake up early next weekend.
10. I'm (OR I'm not) going to work next weekend.

❺

I can't believe the course is almost over. It's going to finish in one week. Most of my classmates are going **to** return home, but some are **not** going to leave. **Rana's** going to start a new job. Misha is going to **take** another course. Masao and Laura **are** going to get married, and I'm going to go to their wedding.

❻

2. hurry	6. doing	10. start
3. going	7. come	11. chill
4. not	8. have	12. to
5. faster	9. jam	

UNIT 33 THE FUTURE WITH *BE GOING TO*: *YES / NO* QUESTIONS

❶

2. Is his father going to drive him?
3. Are you going to eat out?
4. Is he going to study?
5. Are you going to buy her a gift?
6. Are they going to get married?
7. Are they going to win?
8. Is he going to buy a new one?
9. Are they going to take a trip?

❷

2. in two years
3. in three months
4. next month
5. in five days
6. next year

❸

2. Are you going to do something with friends next weekend?
   Yes, I am. (OR No, I'm not.)
3. Is your teacher going to give homework next week?
   Yes, she / he is. (OR No, she / he isn't.)
4. Are you and your classmates going to study together tomorrow?
   Yes, we are. (OR No, we aren't.)
5. Are you going to watch TV tonight?
   Yes, I am. (OR No, I'm not.)
6. Is the post office going to be open tomorrow?
   Yes, it is. (OR No, it isn't.)
7. Are your friends going to play cards with you next Saturday?
   Yes, they are. (OR No, they aren't.)
8. Are you and your family going to spend time together next weekend?
   Yes, we are. (OR No, we aren't.)
9. Is the weather going to be good tomorrow?
   Yes, it is. (OR No, it isn't.)
10. Are you going to take a trip next month?
    Yes, I am. (OR No, I'm not.)
11. Are your parents going to move next year?
    Yes, they are. (OR No, they aren't.)
12. Are you going to be busy next week?
    Yes, I am. (OR No, I'm not.)

4

MARY: Hi, Annie. It's Grandma. How are you?

ANNIE: Okay. Grandma, are you going to visit us this weekend?

MARY: No, **I'm not**. **I'm** going to visit Uncle Steve.

ANNIE: **Is** Grandpa going to go with you?

MARY: Yes, **he is**. Why?

ANNIE: Because I'm bored. Mom has a new job, and we never do anything fun.

MARY: Let me talk to your mother.

ANNIE: She isn't here. **She's** going **to be** late tonight. Do you want to talk to Jeremy?

MARY: Why? Where's your Dad? **Is he** going to be late tonight too?

ANNIE: Yeah. They're both going to come home late.

MARY: Well, don't worry. I'm **going to** talk to both of them.

5

2. same
3. day
4. Actually
5. It's
6. Are
7. am
8. be
9. Is
10. going
11. I'm
12. isn't

UNIT 34 THE FUTURE WITH *BE GOING TO*: *WH-* QUESTIONS

1

(Answers will vary.)

2

2. How
3. When
4. Who
5. Where
6. Who
7. Why
8. What

3

2. What are the two people in the car going to do?
   They're going to play tennis.
3. Who is going to take the woman's wallet?
   The man in the black shirt.
4. What is the man in the black shirt going to take?
   The woman's wallet.
5. How is the woman going to feel?
   Angry.
6. Why is the man in the hat going to go into the store?
   Because he's going to buy a pair of shoes.
7. Where are the people in line going to go?
   Into the movie theater.
8. When is the movie going to start?
   In ten minutes.

4

2. Who are they going to invite?
3. What are you going to buy?
4. How are you going to get there?
5. Where is she going to go?
6. Who's going to clean it?

5

A: Did you hear the news? Amanda's pregnant.

B: Really? When is she going to have the baby?

A: At the end of January. She's going to stop working in the middle of December.

B: Why is she **going to** stop working?

A: Because **she's** going to be very busy with the baby.

B: How are **she and Josh** going to have enough money?

A: Josh has a good job.

B: What **are** she and Josh going to name the baby?

A: I have no idea.

B: Where **are** they going to live? Their apartment is so small.

A: I think they're going to move.

6

2. How
3. say
4. You're
5. marry
6. took
7. What
8. are
9. have
10. yeah
11. engaged
12. Congratulations

PART II LET'S AND MODALS

UNIT 35 SUGGESTIONS: *LET'S . . . , WHY DON'T WE . . . ?*

1

2. f
3. g
4. a
5. b
6. c
7. h
8. d

2

2. b
3. a
4. b
5. b
6. a
7. a

3

2. Why don't we watch a movie in class today?
3. Why don't we do less homework?
4. Why don't we play more games in class?
5. Why don't we have a party in class next week?
6. Why don't we stop taking tests?

4

3. don't we go skiing
4. not tell people
5. take a taxi
6. don't we call and ask

5

A: It's Lisa's birthday tomorrow. Let's give her a gift.
B: That's a great idea. Why **don't we** give her some flowers?
A: No. Let's **not** give her flowers. That's not very interesting.
B: Then how about a book? She likes to read. **Let's** give her that new book by Sandy Morita.
A: I don't want to give her a book. Everybody gives her books.
B: Then why don't we take her out to a nice restaurant? She rarely goes out to eat.
A: Okay. **Let's** take her to that Japanese restaurant near the park. She likes Japanese food a lot.
B: Good idea.

6

2. How	6. Like	10. that's
3. terrible	7. don't	11. not
4. truck	8. Why	12. let's
5. do	9. contributions	

UNIT REQUESTS: *I WOULD LIKE . . . ;* INVITATIONS: *WOULD YOU LIKE . . . ?*

1

2. Yes, I'd love to. (OR Sorry, I can't.)
3. Yes, I'd love to. (OR Sorry, I can't.)
4. Yes, please. (OR No, thank you.)
5. Yes, I'd love to. (OR Sorry, I can't.)
6. Yes, please. (OR No, thank you.)
7. Yes, please. (OR No, thank you.)

2

2. Do	4. Would	6. Do
3. Do	5. Would	7. Would

3

2. We'd like to buy two tickets.
3. Would you like to go to the soccer game with me?
4. José would like some CDs for his birthday.
5. The children would like some pizza.
6. Would you and your friends like to have dinner with us?
7. The teacher would like to talk to you.
8. Would you like to go shopping with us?

4

3. I'd like a bagel and some orange juice.
4. Would you like a piece of chocolate?
5. Would you like to meet us for dinner?
6. I'd like to get a new car.
7. Would you like something to eat from the school cafeteria?
8. Would you like to go for coffee after class?

5

A: So where would you like to go on our honeymoon?
B: I don't know. **I'd** like to go to a lot of different places.
A: **Would** you like to go somewhere far away, maybe to another country?
B: I'm not sure. I'd like **to go** somewhere different, but we only have ten days.
A: Well, what about Mexico? That's not far away, and it's a different country
B: **Do** you like Mexican food?
A: Oh, yeah. I like it a lot.
B: Okay. So where **would you** like to go in Mexico? There are many interesting things to see.
A: I don't know. Why don't we talk to your friend, the travel agent?
B: Good idea. Would you like **to call** now?
A: No. Let's do it tomorrow.

6

2. Would	6. like	10. Sure
3. I'd	7. what	11. break
4. Do	8. We'd	12. are
5. Let's	9. guys	

UNIT NECESSITY: *MUST* AND *HAVE TO*

❶

(Answers will vary.)

❷

3. The teacher doesn't have to clean the room.
4. Some students have to do extra homework.
5. I don't have to sit near the board.
6. We have to speak English in class.
7. I have to bring my books to class.
8. The teacher doesn't have to work during the school vacation.
9. Lunch has to be at 12:00.

❸

3. have to hit
4. have to move
5. don't have to wear
6. have to run
7. have to be
8. have to use
9. don't have to have
10. don't have to hit

❹

3. People mustn't touch the paintings.
4. People mustn't eat or drink.
5. People must be quiet.
6. People mustn't write in the books.
7. People must wear a seat belt.
8. People mustn't use cell phones.

❺

3. Does your mother have to wash your clothes?
   Yes, she does. (OR No, she doesn't.)
4. What do you have to do at home?
   (Answers will vary.)
5. Do you have to give your parents money?
   Yes, I do. (OR No, I don't.)
6. Do your parents have to give you money?
   Yes, they do. (OR No, they don't.)
7. How many hours a week does your father have to work?
   (Answers will vary.)
8. Do you have to cook for yourself?
   Yes, I do. (OR No, I don't.)

❻

A: How's your new school? Do you have to follow a lot of new rules?
B: Oh, yeah. The worst is that we must **be** there early—at 8:00 AM. That means I have to leave home at 6:30, and my mother **has** to drive me. She's not happy.
A: **Does** she **have to** pick you up?
B: No, she **doesn't**. I take the bus home. The good thing is that I **don't have to** wear a uniform to this school. I can wear jeans and a t-shirt.
A: What about homework? Do you have a lot?
B: Of course. And I **mustn't** forget it, or I **have to** stay after school for two hours.

UNIT ADVICE: *SHOULD / SHOULDN'T*

❶

2. a wedding
3. an interview
4. a campsite
5. the beach
6. an interview
7. a wedding
8. a campsite

❷

3. You shouldn't drink a lot of soda.
4. You shouldn't eat a lot of ice cream.
5. You should eat a lot of fruit.
6. You should brush your teeth after every meal.
7. You should exercise.
8. You shouldn't sleep only two or three hours a night.

❸

2. have to, should
3. should, have to
4. should, have to

❹

2. shouldn't, don't have to
3. don't have to, shouldn't
4. shouldn't, don't have to

5

2. Should Mark come
3. should we send
4. should there be
5. Should we have
6. we should have
7. we should serve
8. we shouldn't make
9. should the party be
10. we shouldn't say

6

1. **B:** I think you **should**.
2. **A:** You **should try** to speak English more.
3. **B:** She should **get** another one.
4. **A:** You **shouldn't** sleep in class.
5. **A:** What **should we** study for the test?

7

2. I'd
3. It's
4. too
5. mind
6. wondering
7. graduate
8. guess
9. agree
10. should
11. don't
12. need